WINDING DOWN

*The Revolutionary War Letters of
Lieutenant Benjamin Gilbert
of Massachusetts, 1780–1783*

WINDING DOWN

THE REVOLUTIONARY WAR LETTERS
OF
LIEUTENANT BENJAMIN GILBERT
OF
MASSACHUSETTS, 1780–1783

from his original manuscript letterbook in

The William L. Clements Library

Ann Arbor, Michigan

EDITED BY

JOHN SHY

The University of Michigan Press · The William L. Clements Library

LIBRARY OF CONGRESS CATALOGING-IN-PUBLICATION DATA

Gilbert, Benjamin, 1755–1828
Winding down: the Revolutionary War letters of Lieutenant
Benjamin Gilbert of Massachusetts, 1780–1783: from his original
manuscript letterbook in the William L. Clements Library, Ann Arbor,
Michigan / edited by John Shy.
p.   cm.
Bibliography: p.
ISBN 0–472–10112–9
1. Gilbert, Benjamin, 1755–1828—Correspondence. 2. United
States—History—Revolution, 1775–1783—Personal narratives.
3. Massachusetts—History—Revolution, 1775–1783—Personal
narratives. 4. Soldiers—Massachusetts—Correspondence.
I. Shy, John W.   II. William L. Clements Library.   III. Title.
E263.M4G45   1989
973.3'8—dc19   88–30044

CONTENTS

MAPS AND ILLUSTRATIONS

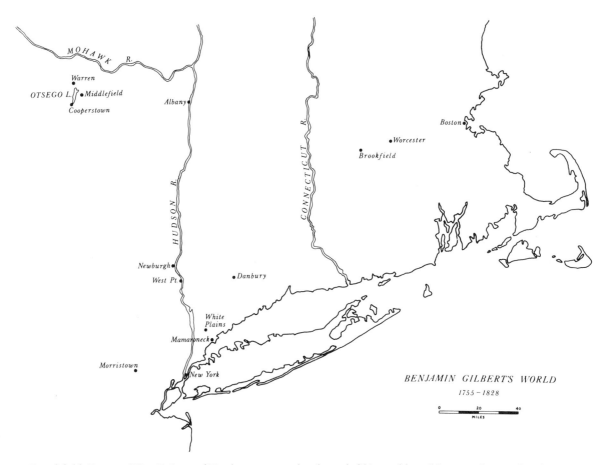

BENJAMIN GILBERT'S WORLD

1755 – 1828

Brookfield, Boston, West Point, and Danbury more or less bounded his world until he moved west after the war to Middlefield, near Otsego Lake. Drawn by David Bosse.

INTRODUCTION

THE WARTIME LETTERBOOK (1780–83) of Benjamin Gilbert (1755–1828) is a valuable historical document. It is a rare window into the mind of a young New England soldier who had risen slowly through the ranks of a Continental regiment, from teen-aged minuteman in 1775 to a subaltern officer of light infantry by 1780 when the letterbook begins. In these copies, faithfully kept in a notebook, of letters written to his father, friends, fellow officers, and relatives, Gilbert gives us a chance to see what was on his mind as the Revolutionary War wound down to its less than dramatic end in 1783.

This last phase of the war—the years of American disaster in Georgia and South Carolina, Benedict Arnold's treason, mutinies throughout the American army, Continental bankruptcy and declining Congressional effectiveness (despite belated ratification of the Articles of Confederation), an increasing French presence in America, the strategic miracle at Yorktown in 1781, and the apparently endless continuance of "dirty little wars" in the South, along the frontier, at sea, and in the lower Hudson valley—deserves more attention from students of the Revolution than it usually gets.

These were the years of exhaustion, growing frustration, and some degree of disillusionment, less with the Revolution itself than with the character of the American people who had supported the Revolution so enthusiastically and selflessly in the early days but whose willingness to take risks and to make sacrifices seems to have been eroded by a long, punishing war. All of these latter events and this erosive process are seen, in Gilbert's letters, through the eyes of one junior officer. The importance of the experience of this final phase of the war would become apparent in the postwar period, when the fears and deep discontent of men like Gilbert would propel State-level politics and finance into crisis, which could be resolved only by the same kind of men supporting a greatly strengthened national government. As a Marxist might say, it is no accident that Benjamin Gilbert came from a Massachusetts town (Brookfield) near the heart of an agrarian rebellion in 1786 led by his former commander, friend, and relative by marriage Captain Daniel Shays, and that Gilbert only a few years later would achieve minor notoriety in Upstate New York as a zealous supporter of Federalist party principles, antithetical to those expressed by Shays' Rebellion. Gilbert's letters make clear that he had had abundant wartime experience of economic hardships and inequities, as well as of governmental weakness in dealing with these problems. Unfortunately, we do not know what Gilbert thought in 1786 of the direct, extra-legal tactics of Captain Shays in dealing with such problems, but in 1792 we encounter Sheriff Benjamin Gilbert of Otsego County, New York, bending the law to secure the election of the conservative John Jay as Governor. Gilbert, the Revolutionary veteran, whose eight years of active service had made him almost a professional soldier, valued strong government for the same reasons that Colonel Alexander Hamilton (only a few months older than Gilbert) set forth in his famous letters to Robert Morris in 1780–81. Both had learned the rough lessons that the unhappy latter years of war, seen from the field, had taught them.

Besides being a diligent correspondent, Benjamin Gilbert also kept a diary during these years and for a time after the war. Surviving portions of the diary are in the Library of the New York State Historical Association in Cooperstown, and the first part of his diary (January 1778 to July 1780, and January to March 1782) has been skillfully edited, and published.[1] While the diary, taken alone, is a fairly dry record of daily activities, it illuminates the background of much that we see in the letters, and it has been exploited fully in editing the letterbook. Helped by the diary, we understand Gilbert's personal affairs, and can make some reasonable assessment of his character and motivation. The letterbook, read in the light of the diary, becomes an engagingly human document. In particular, the diary enables us to learn how he met the challenges, which obsessed him in 1783, of the transition to peacetime.

We know relatively little about Gilbert's early life (he was only 19 when he marched off to the Lexington alarm in 1775), but we know something of his family. In 1747 his paternal grandfather, Benjamin, came to Brookfield from the coastal town of Ipswich, which had supplied many of the first settlers of Brookfield in the seventeenth century.[2] Grandfather Gilbert had been only one of a wave of migrants from Ipswich, and from the crowded eastern towns in general, to Brookfield at mid-century. Parents in the coastal towns had simply run out of land to pass on to their large families. Whether land shortage in the East and its availability in Worcester County were the specific motives for the migration of Benjamin's grandparents is unknown. There is another possibility. Ipswich was a town wracked in the 1740's by religious conflict associated with the revivalistic movement known as the "Great Awakening."[3] During

1. The published portion of his diary, for the period January 1778–July 1780 and January–March 1782, with thirteen letters appended from 1785–88, which had been copied into the diary, has been edited by Rebecca D. Symmes as *A Citizen-Soldier in the American Revolution: The Diary of Benjamin Gilbert in Massachusetts and New York* (Cooperstown, NY, 1980); subsequent references to *Diary* are to this publication. The New York State Historical Association, which holds and published the *Diary*, also owns another portion of Gilbert's manuscript diary, for March 1782–December 1786; all subsequent references to "diary" are to this unpublished manuscript, which I examined at the NYSHA Library in Cooperstown, and was generously made available to me in photocopy by Mr. Daniel Porter, the Director, and Ms. Amy Barnum. The diary sheds light both on the final year of Gilbert's military service and on his personality, but is most valuable as a record of frontier travel and economic life; it deserves publication in a high-quality edition like that given by NYSHA and Ms. Symmes to the *Diary*.

2. Town records of Brookfield, 1719–70, transcribed in 1875 by John Q. Adams (microfilm of the Church of Jesus Christ of Latter-day Saints No. 868522), p. 143, where the original grant in 1660 by the Massachusetts General Court of six square miles of land near Quaboag Pond in response to the petition "of several Inhabitants of Ipswich" is reproduced.

3. Christopher Jedrey, *The World of John Cleaveland* (New York: Norton, 1979), is excellent on Ipswich in the early 18th century.

the Great Awakening churches were split, unsatisfactory ministers were ousted, and disgruntled parishioners departed for more congenial communities. There is no positive evidence to indicate that the elder Benjamin Gilbert arrived in Brookfield with a religious grievance, but the year 1747 is at least suggestive; the 1740's were years of great religious upheaval throughout New England. We know that in 1752 the elder Benjamin Gilbert was not a member of the new Second Church of Brookfield, in the northern part of town where he settled, but we also know that a year later he purchased the last and cheapest pew of 22 offered for sale in the meeting house.[4]

Other Gilberts were listed in 1752 as members of the Second Church, but they belonged to a different family altogether, which had moved to Brookfield in the 1690's from Springfield. Brookfield had been literally wiped out in the great Indian war of 1675–76, and not until a decade later was it re-settled, mainly by people moving eastward from the Connecticut River valley. These early re-settlers included Henry and Thomas Gilbert, who were granted hundreds of acres of land in Brookfield, played prominent roles in town affairs, and were apparently unrelated to the Gilberts of Ipswich. Even within his own family of Ipswich Gilberts, our Benjamin, the diarist and Revolutionary war officer, seems to have been at a disadvantage. Although his father, Daniel, was the elder son of the elder Benjamin, it was young Benjamin's uncle Joseph, the younger brother of Daniel, who inherited the Gilbert "mansion," who became a "merchant," whose death in 1776 at age 43 earned a long notice in the *Essex Gazette*, and whose sons attended Yale and Dartmouth, both becoming prominent lawyers. Our Benjamin's father Daniel held town offices, served actively in the last of the colonial wars, eventually became a Justice of Worcester County, but died at age 95 as what he had always been—a "farmer." His eldest child Benjamin, our subject, no doubt attended the school established by 1750 in Brookfield, but beyond that he was self taught, and self made.[5]

Benjamin's father, Daniel, served in the French wars of the 1740's and 1750's, eventually becoming an officer. In the town records, Daniel Gilbert is invariably described by his military title as "Ensign," "Lieutenant," or "Captain." In 1774, on the eve of war, Lieutenant Daniel Gilbert was a selectman for the second, or northeast, precinct of Brookfield. Benjamin's uncle Joseph was also a captain of minutemen. For Benjamin to enlist as a "fifer" in a Brookfield company of minutemen in 1775 may have been simply part of expected family behavior, but Brookfield itself, unlike many inland towns, took an aggressive part in the coming of the Revolution, and pressure from the community as well as the family military tradition must have played a role in young Benjamin's behavior. In the spring of 1773—when his father was first

4. Josiah H. Temple, *The History of North Brookfield, Massachusetts* (Boston, 1887), 252–54.

5. On all the Gilberts, see Temple, *Brookfield*, 596–602. On the school, see town records, p. 174, where in 1750 the town voted to support a "School Dame" whenever 15 or 20 scholars came together. Four years later Alexander Stuart was dismissed because "his method of keeping school will not answer." *Ibid.*, 224.

chosen selectman—the town voted to buy land for "a commodious Training field" for its soldiers. A few weeks later the town appointed Uncle Joseph to a committee to draft a vote of thanks to Boston for protesting the British infringements on the rights of the colonies. The draft letter, approved and sent, said that Brookfield would do everything "legal and proper" to "maintain those Rights and Liberties for our Children which were with so much Labour, Blood, and Treasur, purchased by our Ancestors . . ." and asked God's help to "Stand fast in the Liberty Wherewith Christ has made us free."[6] A few months later, the town announced its "utter abhorrance" of the "most detestible scheme" to introduce dutied tea, "by which means we were to Swallow a Poison more fatal in its Effects to the Natural and Political Rights and Priviledges of the people of this Country than Ratsbane would be to the Natural Body." Not only did the town resolve not to import or consume dutied tea, but declared that those who did so would be "held in utmost Contempt, and be deemed Enemies to the well being of this Country."[7] Clearly, Brookfield was a stronghold of radical feeling, and those feelings surely influenced its young men.

After the outbreak of war at Lexington in April 1775, the town demanded public explanations from those of its minutemen who had failed to march or who had returned home from the battle without orders.[8] Lest there be any doubt as to where Brookfield stood, the town in May 1776 "almost unanimously" instructed Captain Benjamin Rice, its representative in Boston, to support a Continental declaration of independence from Britain.[9] The first and only minister of the Second Church, Eli Forbes (Harvard 1751) was soon in trouble with his parishioners when he insisted that God, not Britain, was the primary cause of New England's troubles, and the people of north Brookfield dismissed him as a suspected Tory.[10] The town treasurer, Phinehas Upham, may also have fallen afoul of Brookfield's radicalism; he was summarily replaced after the town had voted to pay its taxes directly to the treasurer of the extra-legal Provincial Congress, and it seems reasonable to think that Upham had refused to obey.[11] The war closed the Brookfield grammar school, whose educational efforts are so apparent in Gilbert's letterbook, and the school funds were diverted to a futile wartime effort to encourage the local manufacture of a hundred firearms with bayonets.[12]

The more than 80 letters of the letterbook for 1780–83, when read in the light of the two long surviving sections of the diary (1778–80 and 1782–86), give us a rare opportunity to assess the motivation and personality of a fairly ordinary young man—the kind of historical personage usually reduced to a name, a few statistics, and perhaps a probated will. Benjamin Gilbert, as

6. Town records, 1771–1800, entry for 14 September 1773. This date, *before* the Boston Tea Party, is impressively early.

7. Town records, 27 December 1773.

8. *Ibid.*, 4 May 1775 and 18 March 1776.

9. *Ibid.*, 22 May 1776.

10. Clifford K. Shipton, *Sibley's Harvard Graduates*, Volume XIII (Cambridge, 1965), 54. Forbes rode out the war as a minister in the depressed seaport of Gloucester.

11. Town records for early 1776.

12. *Ibid.*, 2 October 1775, 4 November 1776, 6 October 1777.

he appears in these surviving documents, is a highly self-aware, ambitious, anxious, not inarticulate, and sometimes unattractive person, probably not untypical of the young American men who fought the Revolutionary War to a finish. It is tempting to see Benjamin Gilbert, with all his energy and faults, as the average white male American Revolutionary, the kind of person who would fight the war and later drive the economy forward, opening the frontier, voting for the candidates of his choice, carving out the American future. Early in the letterbook, the authentic voice of this young American is heard in a letter to his father, denouncing in florid prose the recent attempt of the American General Benedict Arnold to betray West Point, the key post where the Hudson River cuts through the Highlands, and where Benjamin Gilbert would spend most of the last years of the war. But we also know, from the published *Diary*, that Gilbert had spent much of his recent leave, in and around Brookfield, enjoying himself. We also learn, as we read through the letterbook, that after his next furlough, in 1782, he would leave Patience Converse, the daughter of a prominent Brookfield family, pregnant. As we follow this little story through the later letters and into the postwar diary, we find Gilbert alternately both blustering and lying, eventually buying his way out of trouble with a straight money payment to Colonel James Converse and his aggrieved daughter.

Social historians of New England have ventured the opinion that a rising incidence during the late colonial period of "prenuptial conceptions"—readily discerned in vital records by comparison of marriage date and baptismal date of the first child—is evidence of weakening parental authority, and perhaps of authority more generally, as America entered its Revolution.[13] Young Americans, so the argument goes, were less willing to accept parental dictation, and were choosing their own marriage partners, often by the most direct means. The story of Patience Converse and Benjamin Gilbert seems to illustrate the argument, until we learn that Benjamin refused to marry Patience, whose first recorded child was in fact baptized only three months after her subsequent marriage to Nathan Prouty of the adjacent town of Spencer. Whether that child, Lydia Prouty, was the daughter of Benjamin Gilbert, with her baptism delayed until her mother was properly married, we do not know. But nothing else in the record suggests what happened to the child Patience was carrying in September 1782, when her father accused Benjamin Gilbert of being its father; Gilbert himself does not mention a child, even when he calls on the Converse family in December 1783 to arrange his quietus.

Benjamin Gilbert would marry another: Mary Cornwall of Danbury, Connecticut, but only after numerous formal visits to the family of Captain John Cornwall, and only after arduous efforts by Gilbert on the New York frontier to establish a home and a solid economic basis for marriage. Benjamin had met Mary Cornwall during the war, when he had become seriously ill in September 1778 while on active service in southern New York and eastern Connecticut. Eli

13. James A. Henretta and Gregory H. Nobles, *Evolution and Revolution: American Society, 1600–1820* (Lexington, MA, 1987), pp. 107–109, citing the research of Daniel Scott Smith.

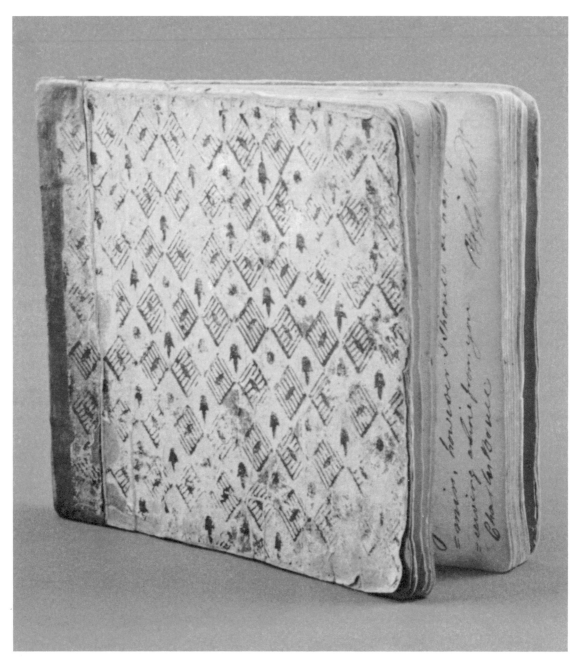

Benjamin Gilbert's letterbook, contemporary binding, half-leather, decorated paper boards, 6 x 7½ inches, 219 numbered pages, in the Manuscript Collections of the Clements Library. Gilbert's signature may be seen at the foot of a letter to his brother-in-law Charles Bruce. Photo by Dale Austin.

Hoyt of Danbury took Ensign Gilbert into his home, caring for him until he could rejoin his regiment in March 1779. Benjamin had been so sick that his father made the long journey from Brookfield in December to visit him. Other visitors included members of the Cornwall family, while Gilbert's recuperation included a New Years Day evening with the "Young People" at Captain Cornwall's home, after which Benjamin suffered a relapse of his illness. Mary Cornwall (born 1764) was only a child at the time, so it would be absurd to charge Benjamin with infidelity in his 1782 affair with Patience Converse.

In his letters and diary, Gilbert frequently mentioned hardships afflicting the Continental Army, particularly the lack of pay and chronic shortages of food and clothing, but he seldom complained of personal, physical suffering. His postwar pension application and published extracts from the Massachusetts military archives indicate that he had been present at major battles throughout the war—Bunker Hill in 1775, New York in 1776, and Saratoga in 1777—although no letter or diary describing his role in these earlier campaigns is extant; and he would be in at the finish at Yorktown in 1781. But by 1778, when the written record begins and just before his serious illness, it appears that this Brookfield farm boy was growing weary. At the end of the war he would confess to his father that his "constitution" was "so spent" that he worried about his ability to earn an adequate living after leaving the Army. Revolutionary soldiering was often hard, boring work, but the record suggests that Gilbert, like soldiers through history, took whatever relief circumstance offered, however hazardous to his health.

Gilbert kept a careful account of both his drinking and his sexual behavior, and from this record we learn that he was anything but a stereotypical "Puritan." The early section of his *Diary*, for the years 1778–79, contains repeated references to evenings in which he and his comrades began drinking and "kept it up," sometimes "very High" through the night; or they drank until all were "well sprung." In early 1778 his tentmate, Sergeant Phipps, brought a woman named Marcy into their tent for several nights, some time later Marcy and several other women were tried by court martial and drummed out of camp, and during that summer Gilbert recorded his own liaison with a woman named Sally More. Perhaps all that is surprising or unusual about these events is the fidelity with which Gilbert left a written account of them. Also surprising is that his son, who carefully scrutinized the diaries and letterbook, and his descendants through whose hands they passed, did not destroy what must have seemed discreditable to their Revolutionary forefather.[14] Later in the summer of 1779 after a period of heavy drinking near Peekskill, New York, Gilbert nearly broke his leg returning from a "high caper" with a group of sergeants. Two weeks later, with the Army on the march, he was still "Very Lame."[15] Whether it was this unpleasant experience, or the receipt of his commission as

14. Someone, probably Gilbert himself, made an effort to erase the names of the women involved; *Diary*, pp. 30, 32.
15. *Ibid.*, pp. 57–58.

an officer, or perhaps simply maturation, something happened after 1779 to keep his drinking better controlled. His diary reveals at least a growing self awareness of the problem; for example, in November 1782, after returning from several days of outpost duty, he recorded: "drank too freely which opperated to the disadvantage of the said Gilbert" (p. 61). But his sex life became, if anything, more active and various after 1779, and is considered more fully below, in the chapter introductions that precede each group of letters.

EDITORIAL METHOD

Spelling and punctuation in the letterbook, as is often true of this kind of 18th-century document, are erratic. Sentences frequently run on, punctuated only by what are clearly commas in the manuscript, and there are many abbreviations using superscripted letters. As far as is reasonable, the printed text faithfully reproduces the manuscript, including capitalized words and misspellings, but abbreviations are usually expanded to the full word, superscripts eliminated, and sentences have been broken and re-capitalized and re-punctuated whenever their sense clearly calls for doing so.

In most cases, what appear to be slips of the pen are left in the text, in part because a few of the letters seem to have been written when Gilbert was not quite sober. The addressees named at the top of each letter are editorial additions, as are dates when placed in square brackets ([ ]).

The notes attempt to identify or explain obscure references in the text of the letters. In identifying friends, relatives, and men serving in the Army with Gilbert, such frequent use has been made of several items that it may be assumed, where specific sources are not cited so as not to overburden the notes, that these items, as follows, have been the source of biographical information: Francis B. Heitman, *Historical Register of Officers of the Continental Army* (Washington, revised edition, 1914); *Massachusetts Soldiers and Sailors of the Revolutionary War*, published by the Commonwealth of Massachusetts, 17 vols. (Boston, 1896–1908); *Index of Revolutionary War Pension Applications in the National Archives*, published by the National Genealogical Society (Washington, Bicentennial Edition, 1976), as well as the microfilmed pension records themselves (U.S. National Archives Microfilm Series No. M805); and *Vital Records of Brookfield, Massachusetts, to the End of the Year 1849*, published by the Systematic History Fund (Worcester, 1909), as well as the vital records for other Massachusetts towns published in the same series.

In preparing the notes, another dimension of Gilbert's life, and possibly of the Revolutionary War itself, became clear: Gilbert's military existence was, in many respects, an extension of his family and community life. Officers and soldiers alike were often neighbors, even relatives. A network of personal ties made the Army, at least the 5th Massachusetts Regiment, something very different from the harsh, impersonal military organization that a modern reader assumes it must have been. How far this network kept the Army intact and at war during the most discouraging periods, like that of national bankruptcy recorded in the letterbook, may be impossible to say, but one can hardly miss the frequency with which the editorial effort to track down references in Gilbert's letters reveals yet another family friend or relative by marriage.

The text being available for all to read, perhaps a comment on Gilbert's prose style is superfluous. But there is evident in many of the letters a desire to impress the recipient, using the language of what Gilbert understands to be 18th-century genteel discourse. The same phrases and sentiments recur through series of letters, and the effect is often the opposite of what Gilbert surely intended; his fine feelings expressed pretentiously and often ungrammatically seem only ludicrous. Royall Tyler, a former American officer, wrote and soon after the war produced the first American stage comedy, *The Contrast*, a great success and an enduring classic of American theatre.[16] In contrasting the virtuous American Colonel Manly with the foppish Dimple, whose sense of language and propriety are derived from the popular *Letters* of Lord Chesterfield, Tyler seems to have been warning young heroes like Gilbert against their own worst impulses. Throughout his letters, Gilbert seems at pains to disguise what he so clearly was—a rustic Yankee farm boy—and to acquire all the gentlemanly attributes as he dimly perceived them. In this respect, Gilbert was part of a larger process, in which many Continental officers were discarding the role of simple republican warriors, and instead began to imitate, in speech and behavior, the manners of their aristocratic European military counterparts, with some unhappy political consequences. Charles Royster has explored the wartime alienation of the Continental Army from the American public;[17] traditionally, Congress and the civilians get most of the blame for failing to support the army, but surely the typical officer's attitude, mixing endless appeals to military "honor" with a good deal of self-pity, evident in Gilbert's letters, was an important part of this growing civil-military tension. At the end of the war, killing time at the New Windsor encampment, Gilbert would record in his diary a whole day spent reading the *Letters* of Lord Chesterfield (diary entry for 13 August 1783, p. 115).

On the first two manuscript pages of the letterbook is a rough table of contents. It is probable that this was done by the author's son Daniel, whose note appears at the end of the letterbook, below. Because the table of contents adds nothing to the letterbook, it is not here reproduced. The letters naturally group themselves into five phases of Gilbert's experience, and these groupings are presented as chapters, each with a brief introductory account of what was happening generally, and of how the general events were related to Gilbert's life.

16. Royall Tyler (1752?–1826), *The Contrast, A Comedy; in Five Acts* (Philadelphia, 1790).
17. *A Revolutionary People at War: The Continental Army and American Character, 1775–1783* (Chapel Hill, 1979).

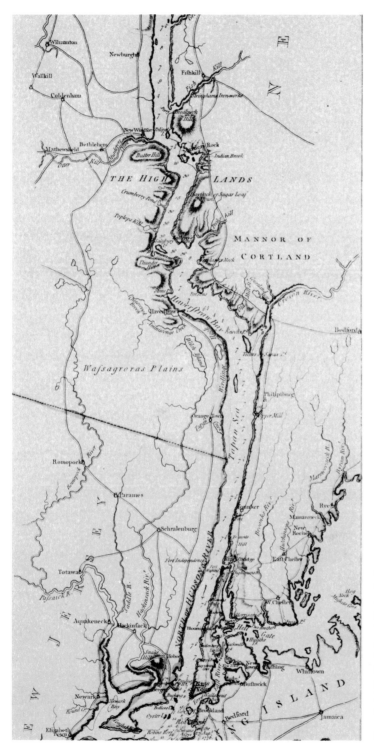

The lower Hudson valley, where Gilbert spent most of the latter part of the war. "West Point" does not appear, but is just below Newburgh and New Windsor, which are clearly shown, as are other places mentioned in the letterbook—Totowa, New Jersey; and Orangetown, Morrisania, Bedford, and Verplanck's "Neck" in New York. From *A Topographical Map of Hudsons River. . .* by Claude-Joseph Sauthier, 1776, in the Map Collections of the Clements Library.

CHAPTER I

TREASON, HARDSHIP, AND MUTINY

❦

SEPTEMBER 1780 — FEBRUARY 1781

BENJAMIN GILBERT'S letterbook begins in 1780 with his return to active duty, this time as a commissioned officer, following six months at home in Brookfield, Massachusetts. After serving more than four years as private and sergeant, he had taken his discharge in January 1780 near Peekskill, New York, and spent five days crossing the snow-covered 150 miles to Brookfield. His *Diary* for these months out of the Army records a round of visits from and to friends and relatives, whole Sundays spent "at meeting," a wedding, a couple of funerals, town meetings, dancing, singing, and drinking parties, but surprisingly little hard work. He had spent a few winter days bringing in loads of the indispensable firewood, a day or two preparing flax for spinning, more days in the spring and summer hauling stones, plowing, planting and hoeing corn, cutting brush, and mending fences, yet the general sense conveyed by the record of daily activity is of ample leisure to indulge his sociable impulses; work, when it is mentioned at all, was often confined to a morning or afternoon, with a social encounter to balance the day. The expected grinding toil of agricultural life is nowhere evident in the *Diary*. During his last ten days at home, Gilbert spent two mornings mowing grass, an afternoon raking hay, and another afternoon at a neighbor's house-raising; he spent the rest of his time doing errands and generally enjoying himself.

At home, the war intruded only when first his commission, then orders to report for duty, arrived; or when he observed local militia units drilling and enlisting from their ranks short-service replacements for the Continental Army; or when a ten-day trip to Boston cost him $1,400. Skyrocketing inflation had virtually destroyed the purchasing power of Continental currency by early 1780, so that Gilbert paid enormous sums (or incurred enormous debts) for what he needed—$210 for a pair of boots, £90 for a sword—or else bartered for it—six pounds of rice for a pair of gloves. With rapidly diminishing power to pay for the goods and services vital to waging war, the Continental Congress could do little, except beg and exhort, to support the Army that Gilbert rejoined in August 1780. We readily comprehend in this first section of letters the continual theme of hardship and deprivation if we recall the underlying financial crisis.

Depression of spirit, more than physical suffering, is the dominant tone of the first letters home. It appears in the petulance of his complaints to sister and father about their failure to write, and it sounds loudly in the October letters to Rufus Hamilton and Daniel Newhall, with their extravagant claims of friendship. The shock of Benedict Arnold's treason came almost as a stimulant, providing (with the exposure of his plot) "the most convincing proof that the liberties of america is the object of divine protection." But Gilbert's mood is generally gloomy, as when he notes the resignation from the Army of his friend and former commander, Captain Daniel Shays, which Gilbert sees as symptomatic of the declining American will to persevere in the cause. Even Gilbert himself, tired of the old army routine, swore "not to be a drill sergeant always"—training short-service recruits, only to have them leave for home as soon as he had turned them into real soldiers. He praised the southern States for what he thought were their superior methods of raising men for the war, and criticized his native New England.

The rising wave of discontent in the northern army finally burst forth in mutiny that swept through the Pennsylvania regiments stationed near Morristown, New Jersey. Gilbert's digest of the reports reaching West Point is a fairly accurate account of what actually happened, except for its emphasis on the readiness of the mutineers as well as other unhappy American soldiers to defect to the British in New York. Not even the British commander-in-chief was so sanguine, and in fact the mutineers took extreme measures to prove their basic loyalty, turning two British agents in for trial and hanging. Gilbert provided an eye-witness account when a short time afterward New Jersey regiments followed the Pennsylvanians; Gilbert's regiment was one of those who surrounded the New Jersey mutineers, and he watched as two of their leaders were shot.

The war against the British does not play a major part in this first group of letters. The real war was then being fought in North and South Carolina, where a British army under General Cornwallis had captured Charleston and its large garrison, and then defeated the victor of Saratoga, General Horatio Gates, virtually destroying the small American army under his command. Gilbert seems hardly aware of this war in the South, although clearly he knew that the war was going badly. A daring American surprise attack in the lower Bronx made a stronger impression on the enemy than it did on Gilbert, who thought that it had "turned out Verily little in our favour"; more affecting to him was the death in the raid of his friend, Ensign Jonathan Thompson of Brimfield.

The war was about to take a sudden, decisive turn, but there is no hint in these letters that Ensign Gilbert anticipated or predicted it. Instead, his personal depression on returning to active duty—familiar to many who have returned to military service from furlough, or even to school from a long vacation—seems a fair expression of the national mood on the eve of Yorktown.

[14 September 1780]

Dear Sister,

Being at this time a great distance from you, and not knowing what has or may befall you I shall give myself the plasure (which pleasure I consider as my duty) at all times to keep a corrispond with one so near and dear to me. And tho you have never given your self the trouble of Writing nor me the plasure of Reading a line from you, yet I shall allways embrace an oppertunity presenting itself with the greatest satisfaction. The kindness you shew to me while I was at my Farthers, has imprinted in my Breast such a sence of your Goodness that I hope I may never be left to Brand myself with Ingratitude should I be so lost to a sence of duty as to do or act any thing worthy your Censure. I should upon a mature consideration there of be thrown under an Infinite degre of remorse and sorrow. I shall allways make it a point of duty to pray for your peace and Welfare at the same time recommending it to you to bear in mind my last adivice to you so long as that shall seem reasonable and prefer a clear Consince to the praises or Censures of Mankind, and to keep seecreet those thing which was my desire, and inform mary[19] from this that my Effections for her are equally the same, tho not Exprest to her personally.

Steenrapie[20]   September 14th – [17]80

[14 September 1780]

Honoured Parents

Should I neglect to Imbrace this oppertunity you could Justly tax me with a breach of duty and consequent neglect and think that all the favors I have received at your hand were slighted and treated with neglect, that when I was out of your sight I forgot to pay that obedience and duty which every Child ows to his parrents. But altho I have not received a line from you sin[c]e I left Brookfield yet I have and shall continue to Imbrace every oppertunity. I impute your not Writing to want of oppertunity or that they have miscarried and shall content myself with

18. Esther Gilbert was born 1762.
19. Sister Mary Gilbert, age 15.
20. Steenrapie was the site of Washington's headquarters in September 1780, near Morristown, in northern New Jersey.
21. Daniel Gilbert had married Lucy Barnes (1728–1772), Benjamin's mother, who died giving birth to twins Hannah and Abigail; he then married Elizabeth Gott (1736–1777); and finally Mary Goddard Kimball (1728–1818), a widow and the stepmother by her previous marriage of Aaron Kimball, a friend and frequent correspondent of Benjamin Gilbert.

Writing till I can hear Verbally or by the Pen. I refer you for news to Colonel Putnam[22] who is much better able to give you a Just account than myself.

Steenrapie   September 14th [17]80   No. 3d

TO HIS FATHER AND STEPMOTHER

Orange Town[23]   October 8th [17]80

Honored Parents

Yours of the 24th of August I received yesterday (it being the first and all I have received since I left Brookfield). In it I find you are all well which gives me singular satisfaction. The situation of our army at this time is not so agreable as I could wish, we being destitute either of Beef, Bred or salt, not being able to obtain these three articles at one time. Not withstanding those Inconveniences, I have injoyed a good measure of health as yet. But before I proceed any further I must give way to some thing that shocks my Imagination. To give it a name, TREASON of the blackest dye was discovered on the 25th of last month.[24] General Arnold who commanded at West Point, lost to every sentiment of *honour* of private and publick obligation, was about to deliver up that important post into the Enemy. Such an event must have given the American cause a deadly wound if not a fatal stab. Happily the treason has ben timely discovered to prevent the fatal misfortune. The providential trane of sircumstances which leat to it affords the most convincing proof that the liberties of america is the object of divine protection. Our Enemies dispairing of carrying their point by force they are practicing every base *art* to affect by bribery and corruption what they cannot accomplish in a manly way. Arnold has made his Escape to the Enemy but major Andrie a Adjutant General to the British Army who came to negotiate with arnold was made a prisoner on his return to New York and de[e]med a spy by a bord of General Officers and Executed the 2d Instant. One Smith[25] an

22. Rufus Putnam (1738–1824), soldier, surveyor, and later a leader of the Ohio Company which colonized the area around Marietta. Putnam came to Brookfield in his teens as an apprentice, and by the Revolution appears to have been a close friend of the Gilbert family. After the war, he taught Benjamin surveying. See Gilbert's manuscript diary for 16–20 March 1784.

23. Orange Town is today the southern tip of Rockland County, NY, near the western end of the Tappan Zee Bridge of the New York Thruway.

24. The treason of Benedict Arnold, while commanding the American post at West Point, and the role played in the affair by the British Major John André, are well known. Arnold escaped to serve later in the war as a General in British service, while André, captured by the

Americans out of military uniform, was hanged. Howard H. Peckham, *Treason of the Blackest Dye* (Ann Arbor, 1958), contains a facsimile, with editorial commentary, of the encoded letter from Arnold to General Clinton that set up the fatal meeting with André. The words of the title, identical to those in Gilbert's letter, are from Washington's General Order, announcing discovery of the plot.

25. Joshua Hett Smith, who had once been an active supporter of the Revolution but later had become a British agent, was tried and acquitted of complicity in Arnold's treason. Carl Van Doren, *Secret History of the American Revolution* (New York, 1941), contains an authoritative account of the whole affair.

Inhab. of haverstraw[26] who was confederate in the above plan, is under Tryal and no doubt will share the same fate. Arnold is appointed a General in the British Army, and publickly declares that he will have a Brigade of the Continental Troops with him before Spring. He has sent out hand bills offering ten Gunies[27] bounty to any American that will come and join him. It has so much influence that many have deserted and daily are deserting. I fear the consequences. Common fame says Arnold was to have fifty thousand Gunies reward if he succeded. I leave you to consider the consiquence if he had succeeded. We should at once ben deprived of all communications with the New England State and must have perished or distresed the Inhabitents. But I conclude.   No. 4

TO RUFUS HAMILTON[28]

Camp Totoway[29]   October 13th [17]80

Dear Sir

You cannot concieve how disagreable time itself appeared to me on my first arival in Camp having Just left the rural injoyments of a Domestick life,[30] and obliged to conform to the strick regulations and implicit obedience of a Military goverment, but this being become habitual and familiar I am tolerably reconciled to my present situation. The Friendship and favours I received from your hands in the of the Winter and summer last past has imprinted in my breast the truest sence of gratitude towards one the most worthy among those whom I stile friends. Should I neglict to make my Compliments to you on so favourable an oppertunity as this I Should brand myself with the Blackest ingratitude and render myself intirely unworthy Your Friendship. I begg therefore to be continued on the Roll among your friends and should be happy in receiving a few from you, and shall take the liberty of subscribing myself one our sinceerest friends.

Mr. Rufus Hamilton   BG—

---

26. A village on the west side of the Hudson, below West Point.

27. A guinea was 21 shillings Sterling, or almost five contemporary dollars in hard money.

28. A Brookfield friend and neighbor (1757–1817); his mother was Lydia Barnes, which may have made him a cousin of Gilbert, whose mother was Lucy Barnes.

29. Totowa, Passaic Co., NJ, today adjacent to Paterson.

30. Gilbert had just returned from a long furlough in Brookfield.

Totoway   October 14th [17]80

Dear Sir/

I have long had a struggle betwene a confused mind and my Inclinations the former having ben made powerfull by reason of my leaving the rural injoyments of a Domestick life and being obliged to conform to the strict regulations and implicit obedience of a Military Goverment. The latter has now so far gained the assendency that I give myself the pleasure of Writing a few lines to one whom I Rank among the order of my best friends. You cannot conceive how disagreable time itself appeared or seemed to me on my first arival in Camp, having Just left many a Valuable friend and all those Injoyments that naturely acru in a Domestick life, and forced to encounter hunger, thirst and all the Fatigues of a Military Campain, but the Embarrassments having become habitual I injoy a much greater Composure of mind tho I am not perfectly reconciled to my present situation.

A few lines from you would be much more satisfying than any thing I here meet with. But I must laconnicate the subject in as Pathetical a manner as possible and subscribe etc.

Mr. Daniel Newhall

TO [?]

Taken from an Auther[32]

Madam,

It is impossible for human Eyes to behold your face without loving; and tho my Lips could never presume to tell you this; yet my heart will not suffer the Secret to rest within my Bosom: I am therefore compelled to this manner of declairing it; you alone can complete my Misery or Happiness; look on me with Compassion and permit me to lay myself at your feet to implore some favourable Attention to my passion; Consider, Madam that Heaven delights in Communicating Happiness to mortals. As you resemble them in Beauty be like it in mercy, and save the man who is dying for your charms—

31. The Newhalls were a prominent, numerous family in Lynn, on the coast north of Boston, when Daniel Newhall moved to Brookfield. Gilbert's correspondent was the son of the emigrant Daniel, and a cousin of Lieutenant Colonel Ezra Newhall of the 5th Massachusetts Regiment, who in 1779 had threatened to reduce

Gilbert from sergeant to private when Gilbert attempted to transfer from the line to a clerkship in the Commissary store; only Rufus Putnam's intervention had saved Gilbert (*Diary*, p. 49).

32. The author has not been identified.

Totoway   October 15th [17]80

Honoured Parents/

Duty Humanity and reverence inclines me strongly to have you in remembrance and returns you my hearty thanks for the care and tender regard you have ever shown towards me. A mallancholly prospect at this time prevents my Communicating my sentiments to you in proper terms. The Massachusetts Line of the army are in a dubious and precarious situation and I fear the event. The officers are daily resigning. Captain Shays and Lieutenant Blake[33] resigned yesterday and several other Officers belonging to the state. If the officers had money one half of them would be at home in six weeks. Their is not one officer or soldier to seven that has money to buy a meal of Victuals.[34] The Regiments are to be reduced the first of January.[35] Their will not half officers enough stay to fill the regiments that will remain. As soon as I am sertain that the remaining Regiments will not be filled with men for the War[36] I shall leave the army immediately, for I am determined not to be a drill Sergeant allways. Ever since I came to camp I have ben up at day-brake a dissiplining the levies and every afternoon when off duty on the same or Business. As soon as they are learned their times are out and we must take new ones that makes us perpettual slaves.[37]

Such undissiplined Troops are every way disadvantagious. They cause great Fatigue in dissiplining. On duty you cannot trust them, they will sleep on their posts. In Battle its very uncertain whither will stand having never Experienced the opperations. So the Bravest officer may lose his honour by having such soldiers.

33. Lieutenant John Blake and Captain Daniel Shays of the 5th Massachusetts Regiment resigned 14 October 1780. Shays later gave his name and reluctant leadership to the famous Massachusetts farmers' rebellion of 1786; his wife was Abigail Gilbert, Benjamin's cousin, and the two men were close friends. As a sergeant, Gilbert had served in Shays' company for almost three years, 1777–79.

34. In 1780, faced with imminent bankruptcy, Congress turned over the task of paying the Army to the States, each to pay its own regiments in the field. E. James Ferguson, *The Power of the Purse: A History of Public Finance, 1776–1790* (Chapel Hill, 1961), pp. 50–52. Also highly informative on the troubles of supplying the Continental Army are Erna Risch, *Supplying Washington's Army* (Washington, D.C., 1981), and E. Wayne Carp, *To Starve the Army at Pleasure: Continental Army Administration and American Political Culture, 1775–1783* (Chapel Hill, 1984).

35. Washington's long letter to Congress, 11 October 1780 (*The Writings of George Washington*, ed. J. C. Fitzpatrick, xx [Washington, 1937], pp. 157–67), supports the Congressional plan to consolidate the Army by reducing the number of regiments, but expresses great concern about the effect of the plan on his officers, some of whom were to be forced out. Many American officers were ready to give up their commissions by 1780, as Gilbert's letters suggest, but all wanted some compensation for their services, and none wanted the disgrace of dismissal.

36. The phrase "for the war" meant "for the duration of the war."

37. As death, sickness, and desertion steadily lowered the effective strength of the Army, States tried to fill the gaps in their regiments with short-service (three or six months) levies from the militia; these were the men that Gilbert was training in 1780.

If an Officer has such Troops as he can trust he will rush on with courage not fearing he shall be left alone in the field. Under such sircumstances if he gives back he ought to be stigmatised to the last degree.

If I must speake the sentiments of my heart I shall say the war will not end in our favour unless the principalls of the new England states are intirely changed.

The Southern States are filling up their for the War very fast. They Class the Inhabitants and every seventh or Ninth or such a number as makes their proportion, furnish one for the War and if he dyes deserts or leaves the field they furnish another. This makes them send good men.[38]

The same money that hired your six months men would have hired them for the war if you had not agreaed for a shorter term. But you will find it harder in future to keep officers in field then Soldiers unless some new plan is adopted.

The soldiers seem to be dispised in all parts of the country unless it is clost to the Enemy, which has made me call to mind the following Verse.

> our God and Soldier we alike adore
> Just at the Brink of danger not before
> After deliverence they're alike requited
> our God for forsaken and our Soldier Slited[39]

Conclude etc.   No. 5

TO [SUSANNA WATSON?][40]

[19 October 1780]

Dear Miss/

The fortune of war that has caused our seperation has raised in my Breast all the tender thoughts that a man is capable of containing and should I neglect to Express myself on so delicate a subject I should brand myself with the blackest Ingratitude.

---

38. New England towns like Brookfield avoided conscription by in effect buying volunteers with high enlistment bounties, even for short-service men. The system described by Gilbert of classing the militia, and compelling each class to keep a man in the field, was an ideal in the Southern States not often attained in reality.

39. The source has not been found.

40. That Susanna Watson was probably the Miss S.W. to whom this letter was addressed is an editorial guess. A resident of the adjacent town of Spencer, she had been born in Brookfield in 1755, and in 1783 married Isaac Cutler, a comrade of Gilbert's and the brother-in-law of Gilbert's future paramour, Patience Converse. While at home on leave in Brookfield, Gilbert and Cutler spent a good deal of time together in what their day called "frolicking," so it seems not improbable that Gilbert might have written such a letter to a woman soon to be affianced to his comrade Cutler. See Gilbert's letter to Cutler, 5 November 1780, below.

The many favors I have Received at your hands has imprinted in my breast the greatest sence of your goodness worth and meritt, and at the same time fills me with many a tender thought concerning your welfare.

My absence from you fills me with many perplexities which causes great uneasiness and the greatest anxieties of mind. Should fortune ever be so favourable as to permitt me ever to se you again, I doubt not but I shall be able to Express myself in a more Explicit manner, and prove by actions what I am incapable of Expressing by word or pen.

But for fear I should trespass on your patience I shall Laconicate the subject in as Pathetical a manner as possible etc.

Miss S.W.   October 19th [17]80

TO HIS SISTER ESTHER

[19 October 1780]

Dear Sister

The fortune War that has caused our seperation had rendered me Infinitely unhapy.

The ties of nature and the Bonds of friendship makes me consider my situation to be injurious to me, however agreable and pleasent they may seen to you. And tho my writing to you may seen trifiling or mear amusement, yet be assured that I take the greatest satisfaction in this of any thing of the kind.

I am unhapy in a great degree that I am not considered worth your attention, not having received a line since I left Brookfield nor a Compliment.

Therefore must think myself neglected forgotten or else oppertunity has not offered. Be that as it may I would not have you write unless you are sure of a direct Transmission.

My Compliments to mary and all Brothers and sisters in the most Effectonate maner.

Please to give my Compliments to Damaras Gilbert.[41]

Please to deliver the inclosed into the hands to whom it is directed. If it is not in your power please to destroy it.[42] I am etc.

Ester Gilbert   October 19th

41. Damaris Gilbert, born 1746, was part of the other, or Springfield, Gilberts in Brookfield. She was the sister of Reuben Gilbert mentioned elsewhere in the letter-book.

42. Undoubtedly this refers to the previous letter, above, to Miss S.W.

[7 November 1780]

With Chearfullness I embrace an oppertunity of informing you of my health. But having but short notice I shall not attempt to make a Descant upon any subject, and only inform you that it is a General time of health with the army, and that poverty uneversally reins both among officers and Soldiers. A new Establishment takes place the 1st of January [17]81. Massachusetts furnishes ten Regiments. Those Regiments to be filled with men for the war by the 1st of January 81.[43] I fear you will have Ill success in Ingaging them. Please to give me an account of your success in the silk manufactury in your next.[44] Compliments etc.

Daniel Gilbert   *Totoway*   *November 7. [17]80*
No. 6

TO ISAAC CUTLER[45]

[5 November 1780]

Notwithstanding my unhappy situation I have some pleasing reflections to think that a near friend has made an overture so benign and Eligable that it will not only render him happy in his Domestick injoyments but make him agreable to all around him.

Having heard from good authority that you and Miss Susana Watson have begun a Prelude that will in a short time inclose you in the Indelible Bands of Martramonial injoyments I wish you much felicity and happiness and hope I may be so favoured of heaven as to have the pleasure of beholding you in that Auspicious state that everyone who envies must be the most Despicable of the humane race.

Altho my stars have proved very unfortunate in many instances, yet I always rejoice in the prosperity of others and more especially in that of a Dear friend.

I shall esteem it as a perticular favor to receive a line from you. Compliments etc.

Mr. Isaac Cutler   Totoway November 5th [17]80

43. See his letter to his parents of 15 October 1780 and notes, above.

44. Nothing is known of Daniel Gilbert's adventure in silk culture. A later partnership with his nephew, Wheat Gilbert, to manufacture iron, failed.

45. Lieutenant Isaac Cutler of Brookfield married Susanna Watson of Spencer, 17 June 1783, in Spencer, the town just east of Brookfield. The Cutlers were an old Brookfield family. For more involving the Cutlers, see letters for late September 1782, below.

[7 November 1780]

The former Amity and friendship that Subsisted between us, has raised many a tender thought in a Breast which flows with the truest gratitude towards one whom I rank among the order of my best friends.

I should have ben infinitely happy had you found it in your heart to joined the Army again, but your inclinations leading you to follow Cupid and hymen, and mine to follow Mars it has caused a distant seperation. I know of no other way to perserve and Enliven our friendship, but to keep up a correspond by letter when oppertunity shall offer. One offering at this time I Embrace it with singular pleasure and should be happy in receiving one in return.

Before I conclude shall inform you that Sergeant Graves and Corporal White arived in Camp this day from New York, having ben detained in Captivity since the Undrell Frollick[47]

Mr. J. Field   November 7th 1780

TO HIS FATHER

[November 1780]

I Received yours of the 6th and 15th of November by the hand of Colonel Putnam which gives me great satisfaction to hear that you and yours are in health.

You mentioned something concerning a Shirt that you intended to have made me a present of by Colonel Putnam had he tarried a few days longer. I return you my hearty thanks for your intended kindness, but would have wished to have herd something concerning the shirt I paid Joseph Kimball[48] for before I left home.

I am intirely satisfied with the disposition you are about to make of the sheep you are to

46. The addressee was probably John Field, who had been a sergeant in the 3rd Massachusetts Regiment, fought at Saratoga in 1777, and was commissioned ensign in his last few months of service, in 1780. The reference in the letter to a Christmas party of Army sergeants, discussed in the next note, indicates that this is almost certainly the right Field. He died in 1829 in Providence, RI, according to his pension file in the National Archives. There is no other letter from Gilbert to Field.

47. The incident in question is recorded in the *Diary*, p. 61, and fairly typifies the casual way in which the American forces operated. On Christmas Day 1779, a group of sergeants from Gilbert's brigade left camp and visited the house of Captain Isaac Underhill, who lived in Westchester County on the well-travelled road south from Crompond to Pines Bridge; there they had a dance and "kept it up all Night. . . . In the Morning as Sergeant Grave and Corporal White was agoing from Captain Underall four Cow thieves took them Prisioners and Caried them off for [New] York." The rest of the sergeants, including Gilbert, made it safely back to camp. "Cow thieves" in this context were local Loyalist guerrillas, possibly from Colonel James DeLancey's Loyalist Westchester "refugees," based at Morrisania.

48. Born in Brookfield 1759, brother of Aaron Kimball; both shared a stepmother with Gilbert.

receive of Mr. Packard.[49] I am not so Anxiously concerned about those in Lomiss's[50] possession as those in Mr. Reuben Gilberts. Lomiss being an Inhabitent you can call upon him any time if you find he is like to Breake. However I shall be intirely satisfied with your conduct if you act as if it was your owne Case.

The Troops are Retired to winter Quarters. Our Brigade winters in Tints one mile west of West Point under the side of the mountains. We have Just arived on the Ground and pitched our Tents.

The Troops for the War are half of them Naked not being able to get their own Wood for the want of Cloths.

Compliments etc.   No. 7
Captain D Gilbert

TO AZUBAH BARTLETT[51]

[December 1780]

Madam

Presumeing on goodness which every wheir proclaims the multiplicity of your Virtues, Constrained by an Irresistable passion Due to the merritts of your Exelent perfections and anxieous desire for your wellfare, I make this Letter a silent messenger to declare some few of my sentiments on the following subject.

Having received a letter from Mr. J. Newhall wheirin he informs me of his misfortune with Miss H. Walker[52] an accident which I no ways expected, I acknowledg I was some surprised. But recollecting myself and fearing it would cause some Embarresment in your armour with Mr. Newhall, I took the liberty to wright the following lines: I have so good an opinion of Mr. Newhall as to think that it was done rather through Inadvertancy than any intinded infringments on the Virtues of that young Miss.

49. Probably Joseph Packard, in 1775 a member of the town committee to raise minutemen.

50. At this point in the manuscript, the text goes from page 27 to page 28. Four sheets have been cut out of the notebook between these two pages, presumably before this letter was copied, because the text runs continuously. Lomiss was probably Caleb Loomis, one of 26 men recruited by the town in November 1779 to serve three months in the Continental Army; Temple, *Brookfield*, p. 240.

51. A Brookfield girl, not more than sixteen when this slightly repellent letter was written. In 1781 she married Jonas Newhall (or Newell), the brother of Daniel (see letter of 14 October 1780, above). Her much older half-brother, Dr. John Bartlett, had treated Gilbert when he was sick during the winter 1778–79, and seems to have been a friend. Azubah's older sister, Silence, married Aaron Kimball, neighbor, friend, stepbrother, and correspondent of Gilbert.

52. Hannah Walker, another Brookfield girl, married Elijah Rice, 1 December 1785. John Walker, her brother, married a Mary Gilbert (not Benjamin's sister Mary), 28 February 1789.

And tho the blame may at present ly wholly on him, I am lead to think that he might as well be deemed innocent as many others who have Fished in the same Pond and lost two baits to his one (pardon Madam my Impertinence) but was their none who worked in conjunction with him. Considering his unspotted character heretofore, and unblamable Life he has ever led, I think we ought to over look it not doubting but his future good conduct will more than attone for this one peice of Imprudency.[53]

As his connections in your family has ben great, and more especially with you, and considering with how much Delicacy he has ever treatted you, I think you would be guilty of great Ingratitude to reject his Embraces.

But least I should offend your delacacy by intermedling with a subject which you may say I had no concern with, I shall conclude with wishing I may be so happy as one to see you united to the above mentioned Gentleman who above all others is quallified to make you happy.

Which is the Wish Madam of your friend

BG

Miss Azubah Bartlet

TO HIS FATHER

West Point   January 3d 1781

Honored Sire

I improve this oppertunity of writing with the greatest Chearfullness, Tho I have nothing of importance to communicate.

On the first instant the 15 Massachusetts Regiments was hove into a state of nonentity, and then they weir formed into Ten Regiments.

The 15th Joined ours [the 5th]. After they were Incorporated the Regiment moved into Barracks wheir we are much better accomodated then when in Tents. But the Soldiers are very naked.

The paymaster has Just drawn a few Cloths

(Viz)   Coats not one
                Waistcoats 2 to 3 men—Overalls 1 pair to 2 Ditto
                Hose 1 pair to 3 Ditto—shoes 2 pair to 3 Ditto
                Hatts 1 to 5 Ditto. Shirts 1 to 3 Ditto
                Blanketts 1 to Six Men

53. This passage is especially interesting in light of   See letters of late September 1782, below. Gilbert's subsequent affair involving Patience Converse.

The Hatts, Shirts and Shoes weir good. The waistcoats Overalls Hose and Blanketts weir exceeding poor made of nothing better than baise.[54]

Now I leave you to judg what our prospect is, and whither our Soldiers are not Justifiable in makeing their complaints, having no Coats no in any prospect to get any. Some have had no money Since December 1779 the others have received none since March 1780. The Officers are under the same predicament as to money.

But I wish to be dispenced as to giving a minute detail of our Circumstances which are very disagreable.

Compliments etc.   No. 8
Captain D Gilbert

TO HIS BROTHER-IN-LAW CHARLES BRUCE[55]

West Point January 2d 1781

Sir

Mars that Cruel Tyrant and god of War who is never sensible of an agreable feeling only when Thosand of Souls lies groaning before him and rivers Blood Issue from their wounds. Not being able to make me a Victim to his pleasure has still preserved his mercenary Calling and rendered my situation Infinitely unhappy.

After retireing from the field to winter Quarters my Quarters weir in Tents together with the Regiment, till the second Instant when the Regiment moved into Barracks. But still many Embarrassments occur which render our situation disagreable. Our men are naked and not like to be Clothed. Some have Received no money since December 1779, the others not since March 1780. Our wood is four miles to fetch by warter and then a bad hill which is equill to one mile more. Now I leave you to Judg whether I am happy or not.

And in addition to my troubles, I have not received a letter from you since I left Brookfield. Whether you will not deign to favour me with a line or your Domestick Buisiness Ingrosses your whole attention I shall not determin, however I should be happy on receiving a line from you.

B Gilbert

Charles Bruce

54. Baize, a coarsely woven woolen or cotton fabric.
55. Charles Bruce of Brookfield married Mercy, Gil- bert's sister, 13 May 1779. Bruce died 11 February 1785, at age 31.

West Point   January 3d [1781]

Dear Sir

Your favour of the 22nd November I received by the hand of Colonel Putnam an return you my hearty thanks for the Trouble you gave yourself in Writing to me.

I consider myself under the highest obligation to return my Complements tho they be in an Illitterate Stile, and to Sympathise with you in all prosperities and adversities.

Your misfortune with H. Walker was not Confirmed to me the receipt of your letter which was a disagreable piece of news to me and an Inci which I did not Expect. But I think Miss Azubahs goodness will enervate the Speech of the Vulgar, and time will Errase out the memory of it. Her Superior Judgment and penetration convinces her that you might as well be deemed Innocent as well as others that Exposed them selves to the same Trap.

This world is full of Trouble and no man must think to Stear Clear of them. I find by daily experience that Trouble is as much entailed to a man as Death and I undergo a large share of it daily. My present is much better than it has been in time passt. I was not off of Duty but Eleven days in December last. I hope under the present Establishment the duty will be easier.

This is the third letter I have wrote and have received but one.

I am etc.

B Gilbert

Mr. Jonas Newhall

TO HIS FATHER

[21 January 1781]

Honored Sire

Since writing number Eight I have Received the following disagreable piece of Intelligence, on the 1st Instant the Pensilvania Troops revolted from under the command of their Officers and chose commanders and marched for Congress.[57] The Officers attempted to oppose them, and Called a number of Inhabitints to assist them. The Soldiers fired on them Killed Six Officers and a number of Inhabitints, then Marched towards Philadelphia. But on their arival at the Delaware the Militia turned out and moved the Boats the oppesite side of the river and haled

---

56. See the letter to Azubah Bartlett [December 1780] with note, above. Newhall (often spelled Newell) was probably a sergeant, later an ensign, in the militia company commanded by Captain John Cutler. On Cutler, see below, 30 September 1782.

57. The standard account of the various mutinies in the American Army near the end of the war is Carl Van Doren, *Mutiny in January* (New York, 1943). Gilbert's own account is essentially accurate, except that there is no evidence to suggest that the leaders of the mutiny ever intended to defect to the British, and some evidence to the contrary.

them onto dry Land and set a Guard over them, they then marched down below Princetown [Princeton, NJ] so as to be near the Enemy in case our people should oppose them, and their intinding wait the result of matters. The Congress sent a Committee to treat with them, the Soldiers first proposed to have all the money and Cloths due to them delivered immediately. On Congress refusing that, they treated with the Enemy and now refuse any reconsiliation but all to be discharged the service, and all arerages [arrearages] paid immediately otherways they will march to Amboy and Join the British Army, which you may depend on will be the case for they consider all contracts with Congress Broke, and themselves highly Injured, and say they will as sone dy by sword as famine, that if they Cannot obtain the dues by fair means they will by foul. The Troops of the other States only wait the result of this revolution. That if this does not work their Salvation they will follow the Example only with this difference, they will march to their respective States. They had formed a Junction and weir to march the fifteenth of this Instant if they weir not Clothed and paid before that time. They now wait to see what will be the result of this, and if nothing in their favour either money or Cloths arives you may depend on seeing every Soldier in his respective State by the middle of February next. I dred the Consequences, having allready lost the greatest number of Troops by half that belonged to any one State. But I leave it, and beg god's assistence in this difficult day.

I would take it as particular favor to have a small bottom of white woolen yarn sent me, to mend my stockings with and little thred to mend my other Cloths with and if ever my Circumstances are such as to be able to pay for them I will, but at present I am so poor that I am not able to buy one knot of thread having been destutute of money this four months.

No. 9   Daniel Gilbert   W.P.   January 21st 1781

TO HIS FATHER

[February 1781]

Honoured Sir/
I Embrace this oppertunity to Communicate some important matters that have transpired since writing No. 9. On the Morning of the 22d of January a party of our Troops attackted the Refugees and Tories that weir Quartered at morriscencer[58] Commanded by Colonel Delancie,[59] and Burnt a number of their Barracks took a considerable quantity of plunder and took Killed

58. Morrisania, the seat of the prominent Morris family of New York, in the south Bronx.

59. James DeLancey (1746–1804), a member of one of the most prominent families in colonial New York; sheriff of Westchester County, he recruited from friends and neighbors a band of irregulars, known officially as Westchester Refugees, generally as DeLancey's Cowboys. He was among those attainted by the State of New York, and died in Nova Scotia.

and wounded a number of his Troop said to be about Sixty in all. We had one Captain wounded, Ensign Thomson of Brimfield who made me a visit at your House last winter was Killed in the Action,[60] and thirteen men; about thirty wounded. The whole was conducted with the greatest Regularity, but has turned out out Verily little in our favour, the Enemy's force being more than double the number to ours.

On the Eighteenth of January the [New] Jarsey Troops followed the Example of the Pensilvania Troops revolted from the Command of their officers and marched towards Morris Town in order to Join the Pensilvania Troops. But finding that the place would not afford so good Quaters as what they moved out of the returned to their old Barrack. Their in an obstinate manner determined to have every thing the demanded, and insulted their officers and every one who Came to treat with them.[61]

His Excellency[62] finding that unless some effectual measures was taken the Troops would all mutinise he ordered a Detachment from the Massachusetts Line Consisting of three Hundred R[ank] and File properly officered to march in order to Quell the Rioters. I Had the honour to be one of the Officers Detailed for this Command. We marched marched from W[est] P[oint] the 23d of January and on the 27th by sunrise we surrounded their Hutts. Having four field Pieces we formed in as regular a maner as if to attackt the Enemy. The finding themselves surrounded on every side with a superior force to what the had they marched out without their arms and surrendered themselves to the mercy of Major General How[63] who Commanded the Detachment. Three of the principal Head of the mutiny was Instantly Tryed and Sentenced to suffer Death. One was pardoned on the Intercession of his officer the other two weir immediately shot, and by those who weir their seconds in the mutiny.[64] Then the whole asked pardon of the General and all their officers and promised to return peacebly to their duty. We then returned towards Camp and arived at west point the thirty first of January wheir we had the thanks of the General in the warmest manner.

Compliments etc.

Captain D Gilbert   No. 10

---

60. Jonathan Thompson had served actively since 1776, had reenlisted for three years in 1777, and had risen from corporal to ensign. His home in Brimfield was just southwest of Brookfield.

61. Van Doren, *Mutiny in January*, p. 216, points out that the New Jersey mutineers were "weaker both in numbers and in grievances" than the Pennsylvanians had been, so that Washington decided to strike hard against them.

62. Gilbert consistently refers to George Washington by this appellation throughout the letterbook.

63. Major General Robert Howe (1732–1796) of North Carolina.

64. Van Doren, *Mutiny in January*, pp. 222–23, fully confirms Gilbert's extraordinary story of the leading New Jersey mutineers being executed by fellow mutineers.

A contemporary map of the Virginia and Chesapeake Bay area described in Gilbert's letters during the Yorktown campaign in 1781. Numerous places mentioned in the letters appear on this section of the famous 1751 *Map of the Most Inhabited Parts of Virginia . . .* by Joshua Fry and Peter Jefferson: Annapolis on the northeast side of the Bay, Elk River and Christiana Creek further north, and "York"town on the south side of the lower York River. As well, a diligent eye will find Bottom's Bridge, east of Richmond, and, just to the south, Malvern Hill ("Malbon Hills" on the map, "Maubin Hills" in Gilbert's letterbook). From the Map Collections of the Clements Library.

CHAPTER II

YORKTOWN

❦

MARCH — SEPTEMBER 1781

ABRUPTLY, WE FIND Gilbert writing from Chesapeake Bay, at Annapolis, Maryland, where General Washington had sent a small force under the command of the 23-year-old Marquis de Lafayette to resist destructive British raids into Virginia. Governor Thomas Jefferson had begged for military assistance in February, but the American force sent, as Gilbert's letters make clear, was simply too weak to be effective. British, German, and Loyalist troops, under the command of Major General William Phillips and the renegade Benedict Arnold, tore the James River valley to shreds, burning Manchester and Warwick, destroying tobacco, and seizing ships while Gilbert and his men watched impotently.

What appeared to be a Southern disaster would turn, more quickly than Gilbert had found himself translated from West Point to Annapolis, into a Southern miracle—the decisive campaign of the war. General Washington initially had hoped to mass all available forces—French and American—for an attack on the British position in New York on Manhattan Island, and for that reason had been niggardly with his detachment of troops to the South where the British Army was doing so much damage; in planning what he foresaw as the war-winning attack on the British in New York, Washington expected to be reinforced by a French fleet with several thousand French regular troops from the West Indies. But his French colleague, Count Rochambeau, had no confidence in the plan to attack New York, and secretly diverted the West Indian fleet with its troops to Chesapeake Bay. Stunned and angry when he learned of the diversion, Washington quickly adjusted to the new situation, and directed all his northern forces—French and American—southward, mystifying the British commander-in-chief at New York long enough to carry out a brilliant strategic coup in Virginia. A large French fleet drove the British Navy out of the critical area, Hampton Roads, while the combined French and American armies trapped General Cornwallis and his exhausted troops, who had expected relief by sea, on the south bank of the York River. The outcome was, effectively for the United States if not for Benjamin Gilbert, the end of the war. News of the surrender at Yorktown brought down the government of Lord North in England, and started the intricate, protracted negotiations at Paris that eventually led to peace.

The letters that follow convey a strong sense of how hopeless the American cause in Virginia looked on the eve of the miraculous reversal at Yorktown. They also reveal that Gilbert learned something at first hand about the South, altering his view expressed to his father on 15 October 1780, above, when he had compared New England's recruiting efforts unfavorably to those of the Southern States. Actual service in Maryland and Virginia taught him that popular support in the South for the war was much less solid than in Brookfield and Massachusetts generally, and that the Virginia State government was far less effective in mobilizing people than were the notoriously democratic regimes of New England. Almost certainly, this brief but intense experience affected his later readiness to support the Federalist party with its emphasis on an "energetic" central government.

His observations of Southern society went beyond political judgments. The undated, late summer letter (below) to his comrade, Lieutenant Park Holland, who had remained at West Point, contains a characteristically blunt appraisal of Southern womanhood and its sexual availability. Nothing, not even the hardships of constant skirmishing and marching in the heat and humidity of a tidewater summer, could calm Gilbert's hormonal turbidity.

No letter or diary entry or other evidence confirms it, but Gilbert's obituary in the *Cherry-Valley* [NY] *Gazette* in 1828 said that he had "commanded a platoon in the detachment led by the late Gen [Alexander] Hamilton at the storming of the redoubt at Yorktown."[65] The teen-aged minuteman who had run with his company toward the Lexington-Boston road on 19 April 1775, and fought at Bunker Hill in June, was also present at the effective end of the war, eight years older, weary but presumably much wiser.

65. 29 January 1828.

Annapolis [MD]   March 15th 1781

Honoured Sir

Being at a great distance from you and very uncertain whether the conveyance is sure I shall not Inlarge on any Subject only inform you that on the 17 of February the [Light] Infantry Companies weir ordered to be completed with fifty Rank and file and properly officered.[66] The Ensign that formerly belonged to the Company was on furlough. I was ordered to march with it, as on a Tempory Expedition, we weir ordered to take only our light Baggage. According we took only a Shift of Shirts and hose not in the least suspecting that we should be absent from our Regiment more than six Days and on the 19 we Crossed the river to peekskill[67] and tarried one night, then Crossed king ferry[68] and continued our march to the Westward not in the least suspecting that our march would be of such a length. When we came to pumton[69] we weir ordered to send back for our Baggage which we did accordingly (and received it within thirty miles of this place). After a march of 9 Days we arrived at Trenton [NJ] wheir we took Shipping and sailed down by Philedelphia to Wilmenton [Wilmington, DE] wheir we took Christeen river[70] and sailed to Christeen [Christiana, DE] which is 85 Miles from Trenton. From their we marched by land over to the Head of Elk[71] which is twelve miles from Christeen. We tarried at Elk three Days waiting for Vessels to Transport us. On the 9th Instant we Embarked on board Vessels and made for this place but by reason of head wind did not arive till the 12th Instant it being only Eighty miles from Elk. Here we are shut in the harbour by some British men of war wheir we Cannot get out, and the channels deep enough for them to come to us. Our Situation is very disagreable being in small Vessels not more than thirty five Tuns Burthen and Sixty men on Board each Vessel. Here we shall be obliged to Tarry for some time without we can have relief. Our Distination was first for the lower part of Virginia (wheir Arnold is ravaging and plundering the Inhabitints and Burning all before him)[72] and if we succeeded their

---

66. This order, dated 16 February 1781, followed by implementing instructions, is in *Writings of Washington*, Fitzpatrick ed. XXI, pp. 232–35. His orders to Lafayette, 20 February, are on pp. 253–56; they include the order to execute Benedict Arnold, if captured, "in the most summary way."

67. A village about ten miles down the river from West Point, on the east side.

68. Kings Ferry was the southernmost secure American crossing of the Hudson, between Verplancks Point and Stony Point.

69. Pompton, NJ, where the New Jersey troops had mutinied, west of Totowa, where Gilbert had served briefly in October 1780.

70. Christiana Creek, Delaware, flowing northeastward, enters the Delaware River about two miles south of Wilmington.

71. Modern Elkton, MD, at the head of navigation on the Elk River at the northern end of Chesapeake Bay.

72. Benedict Arnold, at this time a Brigadier General in British service, was commanding an expeditionary force which was, as Gilbert said, ravaging tidewater Virginia. Although American forces in the area were weaker than Arnold's, Washington hoped to cut him off by sea, but the French fleet sailing southward from Newport, RI, was driven away from Chesapeake Bay by the British Navy, leaving the American Generals Steuben and Lafayette as well as Governor Thomas Jefferson of Vir-

then for South Carolina and wheir next god knows, but what will be the event of this Expedition is very uncertain for it appears that Arnold had intelligence of our comeing and sent his Shipping to intercep us in our progress and has so far succeeded that they have blocked us up here. I have no expectation of writing after this neither will it be worth your while to write to me unless you here I am Returned to State of New York or Jersey.

N 11

TO HIS FATHER AND STEPMOTHER

Elk[ton, MD] 11th April 1781

Honoured Parents/

 I once more attempt to inform you of my situation, and health. That we had arrived at Annapolis and weir blocked in by the British men of war I heretofore Wrote. We continued in that Situation till the 5th Instant when the weather being clear and the seas Calm we Towed one Brig one Sloop and two Skooners out the Harbour in order to attackt them and either carry them or loose the Vessels in the attempt. The British Vessels thinking not fit to come to an Engagement weighed anchor and pushed out of the Harbour. The Armed Vessels followed them and returned at night giving an account that they were twenty miles down the Bay. The Transport that had the Troops on board weir ordered to proceed up the Bay with all possible Expidition and on the 9th Instant the all arived Safe at this place and Disembarked and pitched their tents. Previous to this we had had accounts that the french fleet which was to ackt in conjunction with our troops had an Engagements with the British fleet off the cape of Virgina and got very much shattered and weir returned to Rhod Island,[73] in consequence of that we weir proceeding to West Point, but Immediately after we arived at this place we had orders from Congress to march to Carolina to Join General Green and shall march tommorow for that purpose.[74]

 If I servive this Campain in this unhealthy country I shall not Expect to see you under two or three years.

---

ginia to fend for themselves. Willard M. Wallace, *Traitorous Hero: The Life and Fortunes of Benedict Arnold* (New York, 1954), pp. 271–78, briefly describes this part of Arnold's career, but there is a more detailed and critical version in Captain Johann Ewald, *Diary of the American War*, trans. and ed. J. P. Tustin (New Haven, 1979), pp. pp. 255–96. Ewald was a light-infantry officer serving directly under Arnold's command.

73. This refers to the action off Chesapeake Bay in mid-March when a small British fleet drove off a small French fleet, keeping the British line of supply and reinforcement to Virginia open.

74. The American General Nathanael Greene was then commanding forces in North and South Carolina opposing General Cornwallis.

Our situation is peculaly unhappy as the Troops that are with us have not drawn one half of their winter Cloths and received but one month pay for more than a year, and the People in this part of the Continent are not given to acts of Hospitallity.[75] Therefore I think I shall be very unhappy in this Comand, and how I shall furnish myself with Cloths I know not.

Compliments etc.

D Gilbert   N 12

TO LIEUTENANT JOHN SOULE[76]

Bottom Bridg [VA][77]   May 5th 1781

Dear *Jack*/

I now attempt to give you short Detail of my situation, and the affect of Public affairs. After a very fatigueing march we have arived at this place and are Quartered in piece of pine woods, nothing better then the topmost bows, to cover us from the inclemency of season. Generals Philips[78] and Arnold have a frmidable army in the river and have taken and plundered all the principal Towns on this River. We had the mortification four days since when lying at Richmond to see the Enemy on the oppesite of river march into manchester, and burn all the principall whigs Houses and Stores together with a large quantity of Corn and tobacco and drove off near six Hundred Horses and Cattle and we not able to prevent them. They then moved down five miles and burnt warwick[79] plundering every thing Valuable. They have taken ten sail of shipps and Brigs all well armed and mand, together with upwards of a hundred of Trading Vessells all Richly loaded. The Country appears to be devoted to their services, and it is as hard a matter to find a sincere frind to his Country in this part of the state as to find a Tory in the State of Massachusetts Bay. The State have only three hundred men in the field in this Quarter and those only for eighteen moths Except some few Militia. They have likewise part of two Regiments with General Green not Exceeding three Hundred men in both, and those for no longer term than 18 months. The authority appear to be intirely at a loss what cours to take to fill this army.[80] Philips sent some few of his troops some time since to Williamsburg and

---

75. There were considerable numbers of Loyalists and British sympathizers around Chesapeake Bay.

76. From Middleborough, in southeastern Massachusetts, a lieutenant in the 5th Massachusetts Regiment until his resignation in March 1781.

77. Crossing the Chickahominy River, east of Richmond. General Cornwallis, coming from the southward, had yet to join the British force in Virginia, which had moved down the south side of the James River.

78. Major General William Phillips had superseded Arnold in command of British forces in Virginia. Phillips died of fever later in May.

79. On the south side of the James River, below Richmond.

80. The failure of Governor Thomas Jefferson to mobilize his State in this crisis would haunt his subsequent political career; it may have had some influence on Gilbert's later attachment to the Federalist party.

took an Inventory of all publick stores in that place and locked up the same and imployed several men to purchase stores for him which they did with the greatest chearfullness and with great sucess. The Marquis[81] being in Kneed of stores for the Troops, made application for some part of the publick stores but the Comissary refused to deliver them but said he should reserve them for Philips. We have very little hopes of success in this State, and our fatigues will be very great. We have worn out almost all our cloths allready travelling and gaming about and the gods only know which way we shall be able to procure more.

I will take it as a favour if you will by Captain Parks and give an account of the situation and manoevers that have hapened in the Regiment since I left the point, and if my Commission[82] has come from the board of [War][83] to have it sent on to me.

I am etc.

5 May 1781   B Gilbert
Lieut Soul

TO HIS FATHER

Bottom Bridg [VA]   Near James River
5th May 1781

Honourd Sire,

I now attempt to give you a short account of my situation together with that of the Enemies. After a long and fatigueing march in which suffered greatly we arived at Richmond on James River (two Hundred and Eighty miles above wheir it emties into the Bay, and five Hundred Miles from the mounth of the Bay or Sea Shore,[84] wheir we found General Philips and Arnold in force on the oppesite in Manchester wheir they burnt a number of Dwelling Houses and stores and ware houses, together with a large quantity of Corn and Tobacco, and drove off near six hundred Cattle and Horses, we being spectators of the same and not able to resist them. They then moved down the River 5 Miles and Burnt WARWICK plundering every thing Valuable. They have likewise taken upwards of Ten Armed Ships and Brigs and more than one Hundred trading Vessels all Richly Loaded. The People appear all Devoted to assist the british and refuse to furnish us with any supplies but send all to the British. Even the publick Commissaries in Williamsburg have given Philips an Inventory of all publick stores, and engaged to

---

81. Marquis de Lafayette.
82. Commissioned an ensign of the Massachusetts Line on 27 August, Gilbert had yet to receive the signed parchment making it official.

83. Reference here is to the Massachusetts Board of War.
84. These distances are greatly exaggerated.

deliver them and to purchase more, and on the Marquis sending to them for the store for our supply, the Refused to send them but conveyed them to the Enemy. Our publick affairs never looked in so Dubious and precarious a situation as they do in this Quarter at this time. The State of Virginia has not one man in the field for the War or three years and only six hundred men for 18 months, and some few Militia at this time. The Militia turns out with the greatest reluctance and cannot be prevailed upon to tarry more than one month. Philips and Arnold have taken all the principal towns in Virginia and have ben 500 Miles into the Country and no force sufficient to oppose them neither will their be unless the New England states furnish Troops and send them here, for the Carolinais are little or no better than this state and Georgia is wholly Conquered and have raised troops to fight against us.

TO HIS FATHER

Raccoon Ford[85] Orange County, State of
Virginia   June 8th 1781

Honoured Sir

This will inform you that on the 17th of last month General Cornwallis,[86] with 1000 Horse and 700 Infantry after a long march through South and North Carolinais and part of Virgina without meeting with any oppesition, arived at Petersburg, near which was lying the Infantry under the Command of the Marquis Delafyatte. His forming a Junction with Philips and Arnold who was then at that place made them too powerfull for us, in consequence of which we began a retreat and have retreated upward of 170 Miles before them, they moving at their ease without the least oppesition. We are near the Pallachain Mountains[87] or Blue ridge. All the lower Counties having ben ravaged by the Enemy are in no situation to lend their assistance if Disposed. Fradreck County, one of the Strongest Counties in the State and lying beyond the ridg and in whoes care the Conventions Troops of Burgoyne[88] was intrusted has revolted and refuse to lend any assistance, and it is to be ferd they will arm the prisioners against us. But I conclude being in wood and nothing but knee to write upon.

Compliments etc.

No. 14

85. On the upper Rappahannock River, west of Fredericksburg.

86. General Cornwallis since 1780 had commanded a British Army in the South with the mission of pacifying those American colonies.

87. Appalachian.

88. Reference is to the "Convention" under which the British General John Burgoyne had surrendered his army at Saratoga in October 1777. Both sides accused the other of breaking the Convention, while the prisoners were sent to western Virginia. They were being moved northward at this time to prevent their rescue by Cornwallis.

TO MAJOR MOSES ASHLEY[89]

[c. 1 July 1781]

Dear Major

When I lift West point, I had not received my Commission, but Expected it would be applied for, and sent to me as soon as possible. I waited for some time with impatience but neither received nor herd of it. I then wrote to the Board of war at Philedelphia, but am informed my name is not to be found. I Beg you would make application for it, and send it me, as soon as oppertunity presents, as I am injured in rank for want of it.

Major Ashley

TO ENSIGN MOSES CARLETON[90]

[c. 1 July 1781]

Dear Sir

I received your letter by the hand of Lieutenant Holden[91] together with a shirt, and some other articles mentioned theirin. It was a seasonable tho small relief to my present necessities. Return you thanks for the care you took in sending them to me but was surprised I received no letter giving an account from whence they came.

I have wrote to major Ashley respecting my commission, having sent to the board of war at Philedelphia by Captain Parks, who went on that Business, and in return am informed that neither my name nor the Certificates that weir sent with mine are to be found. I beg you would impotune major Asley to make inquirey into the matter and when they are obtained send mine to me.

(I shall not attemp to give you a detail of matters here, but refer you to Captain-Lieutenant Gion of Artillerey who is better able to represent matters than I am with the pen.)[92]

I shall take it as a favour to receive a line from you giving an account of all occurences that have happened since I left west point together with your amours while on Furlough.

Ensign Carlton

---

89. (1749–1791), of the 5th Massachusetts Regiment, served 1775–83; graduate of Yale College in 1767.

90. Of the 5th Massachusetts Regiment, from the town of Boxford; died 1835 as a Revolutionary pensioner.

91. Probably Lieutenant Levi Holden of the 6th Massachusetts Regiment, who died in 1828.

92. The paragraph in parentheses is crossed out in the letterbook.

New Cassel[93]   July 3d 1781

Honourd Sir,

Having a few moments leasure at this time, which I have not had before for upwards of a month, I chearfully imbrace it in writing you a few lines. Shall inform you that I injoye my health, but am so Fatigued by an insessant marching that should it continue I fear I shall be relaxed and reduced to that degre I shall not be able to do duty in the Field.

Cornwallis (after we had Retreated to the Blue Ridg) had penetrated as far into the Countrey as he pleased, and plundered the Inhabitents of all their goods, Cattle Horses etc., takeing upwards of a 1000 Negroes with him, began to move back towards Portsmouth to carry off his Negroes and plunder. As he moved back we followed after, and mainovered round with an intention to take some of their out parties, but Cornwallis is too great a general to be surprised. He has now made a stop at Williamsburg wheir he sais he will rest his troops and send away his Negroes and plunder and then take another turn into some other part of this state. In consequence of which we halted this Day at 9 oclock and expect to tarry two or three days if the enemy do not move towards us, which is more than we have done for more than a month past.

The enemy by the best accounts are upwards of six Thousand strong, and we at most not more than five twenty Hundred except some few militia.

Newkent County[94]
State of Virginia
3 July 1781   No. 15
Captain Gilbert

TO LIEUTENANT PARK HOLLAND[95]

3d July 1781

Dear Park

I send you by Captain Trotter two Ticketts in the 4th Class, Continel Lotterey[96] Numbers 3.781 . . and 3:650. . Lieutenant Smith sends two No. 3:826 and 3:795. Being a great distance

---

93. Newcastle, VA, on the Pamunkey River, near the head of the York River.

94. New Kent County is bounded on the northeast by the York River.

95. (1752–1844), of the 5th Massachusetts Regiment, from the town of Shrewsbury; active in the 1786 suppression of Shays's Rebellion, later surveyed Maine lands, dying in Bangor.

96. The Continental Lottery, which had begun in November 1776, as a method raising funds for the war, is described by the editors of *The Papers of Robert Morris*, eds. E. James Ferguson et al. (Pittsburgh, 1973—in progress), III, pp. 379–380. The scheduled drawing mentioned by Gilbert was postponed for lack of funds.

from the office wheir the Tickets were purchased, not likely to come that way soon, beg you would se whether they have drawn blanks or prisses. If we have ben so fortunate as to draw any prises be so kind as to make the same use of them as if your own. Pray be so kind as to send on the letter inclosed to Brookfield the first oppertunity.

Make my Compliments to the General of the 5th.

I refer you to Captain Trotter for new and remain yours etc.

Newkent County
State of Virginia
3 July 1781
Lieutenant P. Holland

TO HIS FATHER AND STEPMOTHER

Maubin Hills[97]   18 July 1781

Honoured Parents

Since writing my last, the Army under Marquis de la fayatte moved towards James Town, where Cornwallis encamped his Troops and on the 6th Instant, a small part of our army, Detached as a front Guard, fell in with the Enemies Piquet, and drove them into their lines, on which their whole army formed for Action, began the attackt on our detachments. Our Army being at that time from Eight to fifteen miles from the field of action, no immediate support could be lent them, but they maintaining their groung with unexampled Braverey, kept the Enemy at such a distance, as gave time for six Hundred of Pensilvania line to come to their assistance. The Enemies front line at that time conssisted of 2100, our 700 often changing 4 or 5 shots of a side. The Enemy made a violent charge with Bayonetts, and being 3 to 1 they flanked our troops to that degree, that they gave way, and retreated with the loss of all their Dead and two field peices. Our killed, wounded, and missing is 111, some of which Deserted to the enemy in time of Action. The Enemies loss we are not able to assertain, but are informed it is very considerable.[98] Next Day they crossed the river, leaving all our wounded that fell into their hands on the place of Action. After they had Crossed the River the foot marched toward Portsmouth, and the Horse thro the Center of the Country towards Carolina, where we are in Daily expectations of marching. But I dread the march, our men having not more than one pair

97. Malvern Hill, southeast of Richmond, site of famous Civil War battle in 1862. The Americans had withdrawn to this position after Cornwallis had failed at Green Spring, described in the letter below, to trap a portion of the American force.

98. This action is known as the Battle of Green Spring. Howard H. Peckham (ed.), *The Toll of Independence* (Chicago, 1974), p. 87, gives the American losses as 28 killed, 99 wounded, and 12 missing, British losses as 75 killed and wounded.

of shoes or Hose to Eight men, and the sands are so hot in the middle of the Day that it continually raises Blisters on the mens feet.

Compliments etc.

No. 16
Captain D Gilbert

TO LIEUTENANT PARK HOLLAND

[August 1781]

Dear Park

I shall not attempt to give you any perticular account of the strength or sittuation of the Enemy. They ly at York[town] and in its Vicinity. Our army are lying in different parts of Kings County upwards of thirty miles from them, and are daily marching. Our Provision is very Indifferent but the duty is not hard. We are Ragged and destitute of Cash which prevents our makeing so great an aquaintence as we should do, were we other ways provided for. The Inhabitints are Exceeding polite and Hospitable which ennables us to make more acquaintence than could be expected with persons in our situation. The Ladies are exceeding Amouris but not So Beautifull as at the Northward, tho there is some rare Beauties amongst them. Amouris Intrigues and Gallantry are every where approved of in this State, and amongst the Vulgar any man that is given to concupcience may have his fill. The Ladies are Exceeding fond of the Northern Gentleman, Esspecially those of the Army. Daily Invitations are given by the Inhabitints for our Gentleman to dine and dring grogg with them where they are generally entertained with musick and the conversation of the Ladies. Yet notwithstanding these diversions, my want of Clothes and Cash and the unwholesomeness of the Climent makes me anxious to return to Head Quarters where I shall Injoye the Company and agreable conversation of my old friends. Please to make my Compliments to the Gentleman of the 5th Especially Ensign Carlton. Captain Benson and Lieutenant Smith presents there Compliment to all the Gentleman.

TO ENSIGN MOSES CARLETON

Williams Burgh   September 17th 1781

Dear Sir,

On the first Instant, Count De Grass[99] arived in Chesopeck Bay with Eight and twenty sail of the Line, together with Major General De Saint Simond[100] and five Thousand two

---

99. The French Admiral deGrasse, bringing ships and troops from the West Indies.

100. The French General Saint-Simon, commanding the troops brought by deGrasse; his young relative, the Comte de Saint-Simon, the later founder of French socialism, commanded a company in this force.

Hundred Troops. He immediately sent three Ships of the line and Stoped Cornwallis in York River. On the 4th three Thousand two Hundred of the Troops weir landed and on the Eighth we formed a Junction. While the french fleet was In the Bay, they took one British Ship and several friggates. On the 9th Admiral Hood[101] ["Byram" crossed out] with the British Fleet appeared off the Capes, when Count D Grass, leaving three Ships to take Charge of Cornwallis, put to sea, took two of their Frigates, and Drove them off the Coast and Returned into the Bay the 14th without Damage.[102] His Excellency together with Count Roshambeau[103] arived here the 14th Instant Eight Ships of the line with six Hundred troops and a large Quantity of Artilery arived here from RhodIsland the 15th. Two Thousand Troops from the Northward arived yesterday. These embarked at the head of Elk, the others marched by land to Anapolis, wheir they will also Embark. We have two Regiments of Virginia Regulars 500 Each, one of Maryland 500, besides Militia Cavalry and Artillerey. At a Moderate Computation we shall have sixteen Thousand Regular Troops. If Count D Grass does not leave us too soon, Cornwallis must share Burgoyne fate or a worse. Your favour of the 15th of August lies before me. Received infinite pleasure in perusing the same. Shall always be happy in Receiving a line from you as not one Shall pass unanswered by Dear Sir yours etc.

Ensign Carlton

TO HIS FATHER

Camp near Williamsburg   September 19th 1781

Honoured Sir,

Military affairs in this Quarter bears a more favourable Aspect than it has for some time passt. Count De Grass has arived from the West Indias with Twenty eight sail of the line and five Thousand two Hundred french Troops. His Excellency has Arived from Whites plains with Count Rochambeau and has Eight Thousand Troops French and Americans on their way for this place, some of which are arived, the others hourly Expected. Nine Ships of the line with six Hundred french Troops and a large Quantity of Artillerey have arived in the James River. What Troops Pensilvania Maryland and Virginia have Raised this sumer are with us so that a morderate computation makes our strength sixteen Thousand Regulars beside Artilerey

---

101. The British Admiral Samuel Hood; at the Battle of Chesapeake Capes, on 5 September, Hood served under Admiral Thomas Graves, and deserves little blame for the British defeat.

102. The outcome of the naval battle effectively ensured the loss of the British army under Cornwallis.

103. Rochambeau commanded the French expeditionary force at Newport, RI.

Cavalry and Militia. The French fleet has shut Lord Cornwallis into York River and he is fortifying himself in york Town wheir we shall soon lay seige to him. If the French fleet continues long enough and the smile of Providence we shall give as good an account of him as we did of Burgoyine. Nothing but the warmest Expectations of capturing Cornwallis keeps my spirits hight, my Cloths being almost worne out, and no money to get new ones, having Received but 25 Dollars since March Eighty which passed six for one and no expectations of getting any sone.

Knowing the roads in the contested area between Manhattan and the Highlands was equally important to both sides in this war. This map comes from British headquarters records, and shows the area, from Bedford to Mamaroneck ("Maroneck") and the "Saw Pits," where Gilbert patroled in 1782. Map No. 157 in the Clinton Papers, Map Collections of the Clements Library.

CHAPTER III

WAITING OUT THE WAR
AT WEST POINT

❦

MARCH — SEPTEMBER 1782

W E KNOW ALMOST NOTHING about Gilbert between his last letter from Yorktown in September 1781, and late January 1782, except that he was given leave to return to Brookfield after the surrender of Cornwallis and his army in Virginia. From 27 January onward, until his return to the Army at West Point in late March, the *Diary* tells us how Gilbert spent his last weeks of leave at home. Visits to the family of Colonel James Converse on 28 January, 4, 18, and 24 February, and 10, 13, 15, and 19 March, invariably made at night, forecast the personal trouble that lay ahead of him. There was also the inevitable trip to Boston, where he was able to collect only three months of his back pay, but where the company was good, and wine, grog, and punch flowed freely. On 22 March he started back to camp.

From his return to the Army onward, to the end of the war, we have both the letterbook and the unpublished section of his diary to keep track of Ensign Gilbert. His letters suggest that life from late spring to early autumn of 1782 was fairly uneventful. He was assigned to Captain Jonathan Stone's company of light infantry in the 5th Massachusetts Regiment; light infantry were supposed to be elite troops—better trained and motivated, younger, and more athletic. Not only did Gilbert report the company in good condition, but the whole Army seemed to be better fed, clothed, and supplied than in previous years. The effects of the administrative and financial changes made by Robert Morris, given wide powers by Congress in 1781 when he took responsibility for a bankrupt Revolution, were evident in Gilbert's more positive account of the condition of the troops around West Point. Rumors of peace negotiations and of the European powers making a deal at the expense of America elicited from him expressions of fiery patriotism. Only the officers seemed as unhappy as ever; unpaid for long periods, they considered themselves neglected by the politicians and unappreciated by the general public.

On his 27th birthday, 31 May 1782, Gilbert took part in an elaborate celebration of the birth of the Dauphin, heir to the throne of France. His letter to Charles Bruce (5 June, below) is one of the most graphic accounts extant of the effort made by Washington to demonstrate American loyalty and gratitude toward France.

Twice, in mid-June and again in late July, Gilbert served on military expeditions into Westchester County. These operations were part of a continuous effort to put pressure on the British, gather information, and contest this unstable area with Loyalist irregulars—the quasi-guerrillas, quasi-bandits who made life dangerous in the lower Hudson valley. On the June expedition, Gilbert led a small party to the west side of the Hudson, seized "Mr. Cresse, a skinner" and carried him back to the main party, where the commanding officer gave Cresse "a severe whipping" (23 June 1782, p. 16); "skinner" was Westchester slang for Americans in arms on the enemy side. Back at West Point, the 4th of July was celebrated by firing cannon and muskets.

Before the second Westchester expedition, in late July, Baron Steuben drilled, inspected, and praised the Yankee light infantrymen. But soon after Gilbert's unit had relieved the company posted near Bedford, NY, 18 men from Stone's company, disgusted at being without provisions for almost three days, marched off in search of something to eat. Pursued by armed parties with orders to bring them back, the hungry men returned of their own accord to find that provisions had arrived in their absence. After dinner, they were arrested and confined, but a general court martial required more officers than were present, so the deserters went back on duty. Marching south through White Plains, they laid ambushes on three roads in Scarsdale. On 29 July "horse thieves" driving cattle to the British market in New York ran into one ambush, which wounded one man—John Hutchins—and captured another. After this encounter, they marched to Mamaroneck, on Long Island Sound, then northeast to the coastal road to Rye, north to Bedford, west to North Castle (today Mt. Kisco). His unit repeated this counter-clockwise swing through lower Westchester during its second week on "the lines" but without result. The careful record kept by Gilbert of where he slept and what he ate suggests that he and his fellow officers took pains to make these expeditions as comfortable as possible, nor do they seem unduly concerned by tactical security; an enterprising British or Loyalist force might easily have surprised the troops under Stone and Gilbert, as the men sought shelter from the rain in barns and their officers "tarryed at different places" (diary, p. 30, 3 August 1782), being entertained by local Whigs. Then it was back to Peekskill after being relieved by another unit, and home to West Point.

At the end of August the whole army moved downriver to Verplancks Point, on the east side, where Washington inspected it before parading it for the visiting French commander, Rochambeau, on 14 September. The year 1782 was thus principally one of waiting for political results in London and Paris, while trying to remain strong and alert against any surprise British moves out of New York. And once again the somnambulant military routine would end abruptly for Gilbert, not as it had in 1781 with a decisive military maneuver, but with the arrival in late September 1782 of shocking personal news from Brookfield.

West Point   March 1782

Honoured Sir

I arived in this place on Fryday The 29th of March. Found all my Friends in the Regiment in good health. I have not seen Joseph Kimbal[104] nor any of the three years men from Brookfield, but am informed for truth that Samuel Stowers[105] is Dead, and Whitney.[106] Jesse Watson[107] is living and left between this and Maryland. Richard Dunham[108] I have not seen but am informed he is living. The Soldiers have not drawn all their Clothing but they will be finished soon, when they will be well Clothed. No money Nor any prospects of any soon. We are as much in the dark as to the opperation of the insuing campain as people in the Country.

General McDougald[109] has not had his Tryal. Several Officers have ben broke for over staying their furlough. They have ben tryed for only two Days.

Compliments etc.

N 1

[26 April 1782]

Honoured Sir/

An Oppotunity presenting, I readily Embrace it in writing, tho I have nothing worthy your attention to Communicate which you will se by the sequel. The soldiers are well Clothed perhaps better than ever they weir since the war. Captain Stones Company is Completed with Fifty Rank and file, all chosen Men, well Clothed and in one complete uniform. The Soldiers are well feed, and it is to be hoped will continue so to be.

Stephen Witt[110] who was sent on to camp as a Deserter, is cleared by a Courtmartial and

104. Born 1759, the brother of Aaron Kimball, Gilbert's correspondent and stepbrother.

105. Samuel Stowers, age 18, enlisted in January 1781 from Brookfield. He was last reported "sick at the Southward" (Virginia) in February 1782.

106. Silas Whitney, age 23, enlisted for three years from Brookfield in January 1781. He was reported sick in December 1781, and dead on 17 January 1782.

107. Jesse Watson, the brother of Susanna Watson, to whom Gilbert had written a flirtatious letter on 19 October 1780 (above), enlisted at age 20 for three years in January 1781. He was reported sick in Philadelphia in January 1782.

108. Richard Dunham of Brookfield, age 20, enlisted March 1780 for the duration of the war.

109. Major General Alexander McDougall (1732–86), New York merchant and pre-war radical leader, had been arrested after quarrelling with Major General William Heath of Massachusetts. After a long, tedious trial, a court-martial convicted him of insubordination toward Heath, and Washington reprimanded him but restored him to duty.

110. Stephen Witt, born 1754 in Brookfield but a blacksmith resident in New Braintree on the northern boundary of Brookfield during the war, enlisted in 1778 for a term to expire in December 1780. He deserted in 1778, and was apprehended in 1782. As Gilbert's letter indicates, a court-martial acquitted him because his original enlistment had expired. There were many Witts in Brookfield.

it is the opinion of the Court, that the public has no demand upon him. We have not received any money nor have we any prospects of getting any this Campain. We expect to take the field in four weeks from this. What the operrations of the campain will be is very uncertain, but I fear it will not be great. Perhaps in my next I may give you something more Satisfactory.

Compliments etc.

26th April 1782
Captain Daniel Gilbert
No. 2

TO ISAAC CUTLER[111]

[26 April 1782]

Dear Sir,

I could not discharge myself of an obligation to you, without Embracing the first opportunity of writing you (tho I have nothing worthy of your attention to communicate as you will se by the sequel). After Eight Days disagreably marching through Mudd etc., attended with some falling of Snow and rain, I arived at Camp in good health, found my friends in peace and poverty, the Solders well feed and Clothed. Nothing is wanting on my part as a soldier to make me happy, but $C = t$[112] Cash and New Cloths. My greatest Mortification is that I am obliged to be Seperated from the conversation and enjoyment of the Ladies and be Subjected to the rigorous goverment of Military Discipline. A Reflection on my last winters Excursions makes it the more burthensome. Make no great dependence on the opperations of the ensuing Campain. I fear it will not be so great as expected, all that is said is we must take the field as soon as the season will admit.

26 April 1782
Lieutenant Isaac Cuttler[113]

111. In his published *Diary*, p. 75, for 13 March 1782, Gilbert records a visit with Isaac Cutler to the home of Colonel James Converse. Isaac's brother John was married to Dorothy, daughter of Converse. On this connection see Gilbert to John Cutler, 30 September 1782, below. Isaac Cutler had served eight months in 1775 as a corporal under Captain Nathan Goodale.

112. "Cunt" seems a fair guess at what Gilbert meant to say.

113. Cutler was a lieutenant in the militia, not the Continental Army.

TO JESSE WARE[114]

[1 May 1782]

Dear Sir

You cannot conceive how disagreable time itself appeared to me on my first arival in Camp, having of late left the rural enjoyments of Domestick life and repaired to the complicated din of Arms, and Subjected myself to the implicit obedince of military Goverment, but this becomeing habitual I find myself more composed and in part reconciled to my situation, but am not sedate enough to give you a minute Detail of matters in this Quarter. I found on my arival in Camp, the soldiers well feed, and in part Clothed since which they have been compleeted with a full suit and make Tolerable good appearence. Nothing is wanting to make them happy as Soldiers, but money which we have no present prospects of obtaining.

I am as much at a loss what the operations of the ensuing Campain will be as I was when I lef Brookfield. His Excellency has said in orders that the Troops shall take the field as soon as the season will admit, and further saith Not.

May 1st 1782
Mr. Jese Ware

TO HIS COUSIN DANIEL GOULD[115]

[25 April 1782]

Dear Sir,

The happiness I injoyed in receiving a letter from you is easier conceived than expressed altho must acknowled I was not a little Chagrined in observing that you found an Embarrassment arising from the difference of our Rank and Calling.

How unhappy must I be If my Military Tittle should prevent my holding a correspondence with my friends in the Country, and more especially with those whom the ties of consanguinity naturely teaches us we ever ought to reverence and respect. I would wish that a corrispondence by letter may be opened and continued between us, with that Affability and complasance which ever ought to subsist between friends of the nearest connections.

---

114. Probably the nephew of Captain Nathan Goodale, Gilbert's sometime company commander, Jesse Ware served three days under Captain Francis Stone in August 1777 during the Bennington alarm. On Francis Stone, see the note on his brother Jonathan, Gilbert's current company commander, to Gilbert's letter of 1 March 1783, below.

115. Daniel Gould of Brookfield, born 1760 of Samuel and Sarah (Gilbert), lived in Western, MA, in 1782. In his *Diary*, p. 26, 19 February 1778, Gilbert mentions Uncle Samuel Gould paying a visit to Brookfield, and p. 34, 6 August 1778, Samuel and Daniel Gould visiting him at West Point.

The interview you intended, I was informed of the morning succeeding the day I passed through Western, and was equally unhappy that you was not rightly informed of the place of my lodging.

I have nothing of importance to communicate worthy your attention, but shall ever be happy in transmitting to you any thing that may come within my knowledg, that may merit your attention.

I am with Respect

25th April 1782
Mr. Daniel Gould

TO HIS STEPBROTHER AARON KIMBALL[116]

[30 April 1782]

Sir

Stationed in a concavity between two Stupendious Spercial Hills where Nature has excluded it from her most beautiful part. No Magnificent landscapes to feast my eyes nor Verdant groves to ravish my sences, or purling streams, nor murmering rivelets to cool or refresh me, deprived of the Harmonious sounds of the feathered Choir, I walk abroad in hopes of finding some pleasent down, or Shady covert to indulge my sollitude, but alas! Here I meet with disapointments. I am obliged to immitate the faboules Mairmaid and repair to some baren Rock, and there solace myself with contemplating my past happiness. If I indulge my eyes to wander abroad with hopes of beholding some beautifull objects I at once perceive my hopes Blasted. Instead of beholding spacious planes, Vegetable Fields, or beautified parks, I observe one continued series of convexative Rock and prominent Clifts. When I have indulged my pensive thoughts in reflecting on my past plasures and my present inconsolable situation, my only recourse is to repair to the complicated Jargon and universal din of military instruments. There I drown my thoughts in applying myself to that which most nearly concerns my duty in a military calling.

But to come to that part which is more agreable. Captain Stones Company (in which I have the Honour to command) is completed with fifty rank and file all chosen men, Men of

---

116. Aaron Kimball of Brookfield was born 1757, son of Benjamin (another immigrant to Brookfield from Ipswich) and Abigail. He was the stepson of Gilbert's stepmother Mary (Benjamin Kimball's second wife, Daniel Gilbert's third wife). Aaron married Silence Bartlett in 1778 (Silence was the older sister of Azubah; see Gilbert's letter to her, [December 1780], above). He died in 1833.

sprightly geniuses, Noble disposions and undubted courage. Men who I doubt not will do Honour to themselves their officers and the country for which they fight.

Our soldiers are exceeding well clothed and feed, but their remains one thing more to make them peaceable which is money, of which we have no prospects of obtaining this campain.

Compliments etc.

30 April 82
Mr. Aron Kimball

TO LIEUTENANT [DANIEL?] OGDEN[117]

[20 May 1782]

Dear Sir/

I think myself under obligations to return you my thanks for two particular favours, one for desireing me to write to you, the other for promising to return me an answer. That which depends on my performance I now discharge in a few lines, though they are nether Historical, Philosphical, or Geographical, but a Miscellanious matter containing neither Energy, Grammer, or spirit, as you will see by the sequel.

A report has been promulgated of late among us that we should soon obtain an honorable peace, by reason of a general change in the British Ministery but upon investigating the matter, it is found to be a fallacious report propagated by Brittans solely for the purpose of amusing and lulling us into a State of Security while they gather Strength, recover Breath, recruit their army, and refits their fleets.[118] We as sons of freedom must arouse and convince the Tyrants that we see and dispise their delusive arts, and that nothing but a total Independence from[119] a nation who for the space of more than seven years, have been guilty of every barbarity that the basest men and Blackest Divils could possibly produce will ever induce us to make peace. There

117. No officer named "Ogden", listed either in *Massachusetts Soldiers and Sailors in the Revolutionary War* (17 vols., Boston, 1896–1908) or in Francis B. Heitman (comp.) *Historical Register of Officers of the Continental Army During the War of the Revolution* (Washington, 1914), readily matches Gilbert's correspondent. In the *DAR Patriot Index*, published by the National Society of the Daughters of the American Revolution (Washington, 1966), p. 503, there is a 2d Lieut. Daniel Ogden, Jr. (1734–1819) of New York; *Massachusetts Soldiers and*

Sailors, xi, p. 624, lists a Daniel Ogden, a private in early 1781, who had enlisted for the duration of the war and was serving in the 1st New York Regiment. In a second letter to Ogden, 16 February 1783, below, Gilbert addresses him as being in Springfield, MA.

118. In fact, the rumor of peace was fairly accurate.

119. Gilbert revised extensively this part of his letter, scratching out a passage that read: ". . . and renounce them that we disdain the remotes idea of ever reuniting with . . ."

has been a mutiny in the Connecticut line in Consequence of the Army's not receiving pay since the beginning of 1781.[120] Some of the mutineers were confined and one Hanged. Had I any thing worthy your attention I would continue my Epissel as I have not shall conclude.

20th May 1782
Lieutenant Ogden

TO HIS BROTHER-IN-LAW CHARLES BRUCE

[5 June 1782]

Dear Sir

Yesterday was celebrated at this place, the Birth of the dauphin of france.[121] Previous to the feast a grand Colonnade was erected consisting of 120 pillars in 5 rows wound with evergreens, on the top of which was erected four galliries enclosing the main roof. On the top of each pillar was bound branches of evergreens representing Trees in full life. On front of each pillar was placed in rotation Flower de luces,[122] and thirteen stars, painted in various coulers. Between the pillars was hanging green curtains decorated with a variety of paintings. At the uper end of the arbour was the american coat of arms painted in blue white and yellow, and round the coat of arms hung a curtain of green yellow and white and underneath was rote in cappitals Independance peace and perpetual alliance. At the lower end a french coat of arms Beautified in the above maner and underneath was rote in cappitals long live the dauphin of france. The whole Bower was Beautified with painting of various kinds with stars, flowers deluces, chains, curtains, ovels, loops, sashes and candlesticks, too many to number and too curious for me to describe.

All the Generals, field Commanders, and staff officers of the army stationed in this Quarter together with a number of Gentlemen and Ladies from the country dined at once under the arbour. Thirteen toasts was drank and after each toast a discharge of 13 cannon.

As soon as dark the arbour was illuminated with upwards 1100 candles and the troops

---

120. Gilbert was not exaggerating. Robert Morris, Superintendent of Finance, took the position that paying the Continental Army should be done by requisition on the States; if the States did not pay their requisition to the Continental treasury, then the troops and officers would go without pay. Morris, however, paid the salaries of the civilian staff who supplied the Army, and this discrepancy excited considerable discontent within the Army. Washington described all this in his letter to Mor-

ris, 17–[25] May 1782, *Writings of Washington*, Fitzpatrick ed., xxiv, pp. 287–91. Morris was not only saving money by not paying the army, but also putting pressure on the States to support central government. Ferguson, *Power of the Purse*, pp. 134, 155.

121. First son born to Louis XVI and Marie-Antoinette, he died on the eve of the French Revolution.

122. *Fleurs-de-lis* (*fleurs-de-luces* is an acceptable variant).

paraded in single file on the different heights round the point and fird a fu dejoy[123] a 3 different times with a discharge of 13 cannon between fire. After the fireing a display of fireworks was exhibited to universal satisfaction of all beholders. The whole was closed with the discharge of 3 cannon at which time the troops retired to their Quarters. The whole was conducted with the greatest regularity and good order.

Compliments etc.

5 June 1782
Mr. Charles Bruce   No. 2

TO HIS FATHER

[1 June 1782]

Honored Sir

Yours of the 11 ultimo lies before, am happy in hearing of your health, but exceeding sorry to find that all your family do not all enjoy the same blessing.

I enjoy a competency of health but not peace of mind. The soldiers, notwithstanding they are well fed and clothed, are not contented but are calling for money and not without reason, not having received any pay Since the begining of the last year. The connecticut line have mutined in consequence of their pays being withholden from them. Some of the mutineers was confined and one hanged. We are not without fears that the Massachusetts line will follow the example, as they have been promised they Should receive money at the opening of the campain, and now are informed they will not.

The announcement of the Birth of a Dauphin of France was celebrated at this place the 31st ultimo. A grand arbour was erected and an elegant entertainment given by the commander in chief on the ocasion. A number of cannon was fired together with a fu dejoy and the day closed with a great display of fire works.

Compliments etc.

1st June 1782
Captain Daniel Gilbert
No. 3

123. *Feu-de-joie*: a military ceremony in which muskets were fired along a line to celebrate a victory or other joyful event.

[7 July 1782]

Dear Sir

It has been such a Barren season for news that I have not wrote you but one letter before this since I left Brookfield.

There is no great prospect of a Supply of News soon, as only a part of the Troops have taken the field, the others remain in Barracks. I fear the Campain will not be very active unless a French fleet should come on the coast, which we have no great reason to expect considering their late defeat.[124]

It is a General time of health with our Soldiers. They are weel feed, and as well Clothed as any British Troops.

Compliments etc.

West Point
7th July 1782
Mr. Joseph Dane
No. 2

TO HIS FATHER

[8 July 1782]

Honoured Sire,

I receved yours of the first of June and the 25 Ditto, Numbers 2 and 4 but No. 3 I have not Received. I am happy in hearing your family in general are in good health, but it would ad to my happyness to here it was universal.

You informed me in No. 2 that you had sent my Note to Boston and it was consolidated and returned. I wish to here what the sum is.[125]

Please to give me an account in your next what sucess you have had with your silk worms this year, whether money is more plentyfull now than it was when I left Brookfield, how people pay their rates, and how heavy they are,[126] and what Peoples Sentiments in general is concerning the war.

---

124. By April the British Admirals Hood and Rodney had managed to unite their fleets at Antigua in the West Indies, and to defeat a French invasion fleet moving toward Jamaica from Martinique in what is usually called the Battle of the Saints.

125. It is not clear from this whether Gilbert's note was in effect re-financed by the State of Massachusetts or a private lender.

126. Gilbert's queries reflect the message conveyed by Robert Morris, that payment of the army depended on the willingness of the States to raise revenue through taxation of their own citizens.

I have herd captain Shays was one of the Chiefs of the Mobb who attempted to stop the court. I wish to be certified in that matter.[127]

Compliments etc.

West Point
8th July 1782   No. 4
Captain D Gilbert

TO DAVID BALDWIN[128]

13 July 1782

Dear Sir

Perhaps you will be surprised at receiving a letter from one who's acquaintence with your self has been so small. Yet be assured I took the liberty from a Principal of gratitude. The generous and polite treatment I received from your hands when on a visit at Sudbury last winter lays me under the greatest obligations and calls for my humble acknowledments, and could I f[l]atter myself with receiving a line from you in return, my happyness in that would be complete.

Since I had the pleasure of your company at Mr. Barkers, I have Injoyed my health, I am now Stationed at WEST POINT on the Banks of the Hudson, where the greater part of the army are at present.

127. Captain Shays was the nominal leader of the tax rebellion in Massachusetts in 1786 that helped to precipitate the Federal Constitutional Convention in 1787. He had lived in Brookfield, and after the war lived in Pelham. He had married Abigail Gilbert, who appears to have been Benjamin Gilbert's first cousin (the daughter of his Uncle Benjamin). Benjamin Gilbert had served as a sergeant in Captain Daniel Shays' company of the 5th Massachusetts Regiment during the Saratoga campaign of 1777 and at least until his commissioning as ensign in 1779, and in other respects the two men seem to have been close friends. Gilbert's *Diary* describes visits between the two; for example, p. 73, 1 March 1782: "Capt. Shay & Lady came to our House & din'd & spent the afternoon," and earlier there is an account of an all-night party in camp at Captain Shays' quarters where they "kept it up very high," which was Gilbert's phrase for heavy drinking (*ibid.*, p. 23, 24 January 1778). After the war, in 1785, on a trip back to Brookfield from Cherry Valley, New York, Gilbert's horse went lame around Albany, and he went on foot as far as Pelham, where Shays lent him a horse, mounted another, and rode with him to Brookfield. There is also a friendly letter of 1785 from Gilbert to Shays, printed at the end of the *Diary*, pp. 77–78, in which he asks him to forward a letter to Gilbert's "Dada" in Brookfield. Shays left the army in 1780. The 1782 affair about which Gilbert is asking to be "certified" (i.e., more accurately informed) involved a mob stopping civil suits (especially for debt) in the Northampton court, and is briefly described in George R. Minot, *The History of the Insurrections in Massachusetts* (Boston, 1810), pp. 12–13, 25–26. The puzzle in all this is of course what Gilbert, who became a fervent Federalist, thought of the political radicalism of his friend, relative, and former commander; nowhere does Gilbert leave a clue to the answer.

128. Not identified, but the Baldwin family of North Brookfield, which Gilbert mentioned frequently in his postwar diary, had members in Sudbury. Temple, *Brookfield*, p. 502.

We are well suplied with provisions and the soldiers well Clothed but the old story remains good. No Cash.

Lieutenant Smiths Compliments etc.

Mr David Baldwin
East Sudbury

TO HIS SISTER ESTHER

[23 August 1782]

Dear Sister

Tho' stationed at a great distance from you I still retain that respect and Effection which is due to your merrit, and to whom I am under the greatest obligations for past Kindnesses.

I expect to be at home by the last of December, or the begining of January next. I wish you would use your Influence to have my Great Coats Cloth finished by that time, as I shall be destitute of an outer garment.

Make my compliments to Mr. Hamilton and Lady etc.

West Point   23d August 1782
Miss Esther Gilbert

TO HIS COUSIN DANIEL GOULD[129]

[23 August 1782]

Dear Sir

Yours of the 25th of June came safe to hand. Immediately on recet therof I was ordered on the lines, which prevented my Answering it, till the present moment. I Sincerely and heartly join with you in your wishes, and doubt not but we shall soon obtain them. Our public affairs appear with a more favourable aspect than they have since the War.

Official accounts (some of which have been published) declare that a peace is Negociating and that it will soon take place. Should this be the happy case, I shall soon wait upon you and communicate my sintiments Verbaly. Till then I shall expect a continuance of this Corrispond. All matters relative to my good or bad fortune, I shall take the earliest oppertunity of communicating, and have the happyness at this time of informing you that I have received a Lieutenant's appointment in the 5th Massachusetts Regiment and am anexed to the Light Infantry Company. The Light Infantry of the army are organized and the greater part have

129. See note 115, above.

taken the field. The remainder of us leave the point to morrow. The Army is ordered to hold themselves in readiness to move at an hours warning. Their destination to me is unknown, perhaps in my next I can give you information. Till then I am etc.

West Point   23 August 82
Mr. Daniel Gould

TO HIS FATHER

[24 August 1782]

Honoured Sire/

In consequence of the armies being kept without pay this summer a great number of Officers have resined which has made a Vacancy for Lieutenacy for me, and since writing my last I have received my appointment and am continued in the light Company. The light Infantry of the Army is organized and the greater part have taken the field, the remaining part of us leaves the point tomorrow. The whole Army are ordered to be ready to move at an hours warning. Wheir their distination is I can't say. We have for some time past been under the most Sanguine expectations of a speedy peace, but of late our hopes have been blasted by hearing the Empress of Rusha had entered into an alliance with Brittan and is determined to Sink with Brittan or subject her colonis.[130] I have received no letters from you since the 25 of June last. I wish in your next you woud inform me what sums of money has been collected by the excise act[131] agreable to common report and whether the people have got reconsiled in general to it. We have a report prevailing in the army that their is an impost laid on all Europian goods and that it brings large sums into the Treasury.[132] I wish to be Certified as to that. I have been informed that major Harwood is in low Circumstances.[133] I wish to be Certified as to that also. Levi Brown is well and is promoted to Corporal.[134] Benjamin Jennings was will two days ago.[135]

24th August 1782
Captain D Gilbert   No. 5

130. Gilbert here was reflecting the exaggerated American fear that Empress Catherine the Great would succeed in a continuing Russian interest in persuading Britain to let her "mediate" an end to the war at the expense of France and its American ally.

131. A Massachusetts tax on wine, tea, rum, brandy, and carriages. See Gilbert's letter of 18 December 1782 with note, below.

132. Gilbert was too sanguine. Rhode Island defeated the proposed 5% import duty (or "impost"). Ferguson, *Power of the Purse*, pp. 116–17, 152–53.

133. Peter Harwood had been Gilbert's first company commander, in 1775–76. See the letter of 18 December 1782, below, and note. Harwood was indeed in financial difficulties.

134. Levi Brown of Brookfield was enlisted at age 18 by Gilbert himself as a drummer in the 5th Massachusetts Regiment for the duration of the war.

135. Benjamin Jennings of Brookfield, at age 17, had enlisted for six months in 1780. His record of service for 1782 was not found.

[24 September 1782]

Dear Sir

Destitute of a Study, Deprived of a Dictionary, and forsaken by the muses, I remain Dormant Anticipating the Troubles that await me, which I shall not fail of undergoing after the first of January next.

I expect to make my commorance in the State of Vermont under the Tuition of Ceres, constantly attended by Fressonia forsaken by Somnus, while others are in an Ataraxain State under the Auspicious government of Falicitus, and Lubentia, Embracing Comus. These Tenebrious prospects deprives me of all lucid Intervals. At certain times my reason is so Infatuated that I almost determin to Emigrate from my Country and become a Vagrant, but this resolution becomes an Embryo, and I remain absorbed in a continual perturbation.

If you have any thing to divert the mind, Solace or Tantalize me under this Dolor, please to communicate it as soon as opportunity Shall present. Such a Rhapsody as this perhaps never before was presented to man for perusal. I beg you would excuse it as I declare myself your Cincere friend.

B. Gilbert

24th September
Lieutenant Warren

136. From Brookfield, adjutant of the 5th Massachusetts Regiment, served in Virginia with Gilbert under Lafayette in 1781, died 1823.

CHAPTER IV

SCANDAL AND MONEY

❦

I T IS NOT EASY, near the end of the twentieth century, to recapture what a pregnancy outside of marriage actually meant for Americans living two centuries ago, so distant from our own evolving, contentious views of sexual and personal behavior. We are apt to see the issue through the distorting prism of more than a hundred years of Victorian morality, which lies between us and Gilbert's generation, and to ascribe to him and his pre-Victorian contemporaries some sort of vestigial "Puritan" attitude toward sex. But it is equally wrong to assume that Revolutionary America was engaged in a conscious rebellion against traditional standards of behavior, and was struggling not only for national independence and democratic government but also toward the type of sexual freedom that so many in our own era have celebrated. The question is properly historical, in that we can find interesting answers by paying close attention to relatively scarce and scattered evidence of just the kind that the crisis in Gilbert's life created.

On Tuesday, 24 September 1782, in camp on the east side of the Hudson, Benjamin Gilbert learned in a letter from Brookfield that Patience Converse was pregnant, and that she had named him as the father. The letter came from Captain John Cutler, the husband of Dorothy, the older sister of Patience, and had been written and sent on behalf of Patience's father, Colonel James Converse of Brookfield. How did Benjamin and Patience, their families, friends, and neighbors react to the situation? All we know is what Benjamin said and did about it.

From his letters to Azubah Bartlett and Jonas Newhall of a year before ([December 1780] and 3 January 1781, above), we know that Gilbert was at least familiar with the situation in which he now found himself, and could take—at least when others were involved—a pragmatic, more flippant than enlightened, view of the matter. But even without the Converse side of the correspondence, we can see in his first response to the aggrieved Colonel a degree of guilt-stricken embarrassment which reminds us that as recently as 1925 Theodore Dreiser could plausibly call a comparable, fictional situation *An American Tragedy*, and suggest that suicide or murder, as well as marriage, were ways of resolving it. Gilbert himself in his response to the Colonel refers to the possibility of a "matrimonial coalescence," if only to say that military service made an immediate marriage (Patience must have been very near the term of her pregnancy if Gilbert was the father; he had left Brookfield in March 1782) impossible. But

Gilbert was not so contrite as to resist an impulse to strike back at the officious messenger, John Cutler, by signing his covering note to Cutler, "Superlatively yours etc."

But a careful reading of all the evidence conveys no simple picture of how early American *mores* might be reflected in the Gilbert-Converse crisis of 1782. Gilbert soon became evasive, perhaps mendacious, proclaiming his innocence and blaming others, including the Cutler brothers, John and Isaac. Whether he had good grounds for doing so is unknown. Gilbert's father, Daniel, when he finally raised the matter in a letter to his son, seems not to have been shocked or much embarrassed, and gave Benjamin the support he needed to avoid marriage with Patience Converse—assuming that *she* was willing to marry *him*. In the end, Benjamin Gilbert ignored the child, if there was one, and months after its birth simply bought his way out of the difficulty. The introduction to the next chapter describes this outcome in detail.

This matter naturally preoccupied him during his last winter in the Army. His other chief concern from October 1782 to March 1783 was in finding the money needed to buy the land on which he could build a postwar future. Although the town records of Brookfield refer to his farm, and his letters mention his sheep and other property, leaving Brookfield after the war seems to have been taken for granted. Whether the Converse affair figured in his decision to leave is unknown, but in the letter to his father of 30 January 1783, below, he alluded to unnamed enemies who were dragging his name through the mire: "Scandal is such a prevalent evil in Brookfield, that while I have so many enemies in that place who wish to destroy my character, Interest, and Life, could they take it without being called to an account, that no friend of mine need be at a loss from whence all this clamour proceeds." Later, the record of town meetings would show that Brookfield declined to pay Benjamin Gilbert compensation, as was usual, when a public road was built through part of his farm. Brookfield, never overfull of good arable land, was clearly not part of his plan for a postwar life.

Gilbert had spent virtually his entire adulthood in the Army, at war. Unlike most private soldiers, who enlisted for a limited term or deserted when they grew weary of army life, officers like Gilbert, who had served from the beginning in 1775, felt that they had acquired a substantial personal investment in their military positions. At first they had demanded postwar half-pay for life, small permanent pensions on the European model. Then they agreed to settle for less—an actuarial commutation of lifetime half-pay into a lump sum payment. What they actually got would be devalued by uncontrollable inflation, and by their failure for months at a time to get anything at all, either from Congress or from their State governments.[137] Of course they could always get *something*—credit from those still ready to extend it to officers (who were presumptive gentlemen), and cash especially from those willing to buy pay certificates and land bounties at steep discounts, twenty or thirty percent of face value, or less. In Gilbert's case,

137. Ferguson, *Power of the Purse*, is an authoritative and succinct account of these financial problems.

which seems fairly typical, we see how one young officer scrambled to find the financial means of securing his future. He failed in the end to gather the money needed to become a partner in Captain Nathan Goodale's speculation in confiscated Loyalist lands near Albany, New York. As in the Converse affair, his father helped him, but apparently not enough, or quickly enough. But it was less his shortage of funds than the untimely arrival of peace, "thou Darling Attribute of the Gods" as Gilbert called it, that definitively killed the Albany land scheme. The peace treaty of 1783 expressly forbade any further punishment of Americans who had supported Britain, thus ending all hope that the lands around Albany scheduled for confiscation would ever be auctioned to bidders like Goodale and Gilbert.

A surprising feature of Gilbert's diary and letterbook for this period is the absence of any direct account of what is generally known as the "Newburgh affair" or "Newburgh conspiracy," when for a moment in March 1783 it seemed as if Army officers, unhappy about their pay and treatment by Congress and the States, might make common cause with a group of nationalist delegates in Congress to carry out some sort of political coup. Details of the affair are murky and disputed, but on 10 March an anonymous manifesto was circulating among the officers stationed near West Point, and on 15 March Washington openly confronted, and effectively quashed, whatever plot was brewing among his subordinates. Lieutenant Gilbert, who was so attentive to issues of officers' pay and treatment, barely alluded to what historians have described as a serious political crisis at the end of the Revolutionary War. In his letter to Captain Jonathan Stone of 1 March, below, he briefly described the negative response from Congress to a petition carried to Philadelphia by a small delegation of officers. But neither in his letters nor in the diary did he mention the events of the crucial days 10–15 March. Perhaps his mind was elsewhere: on Monday night the 10th he visited the brothel at "Wyoma" (see introduction to Chapter V, below), returning early Tuesday morning, and he went again Friday night the 14th, returning early Saturday morning—the historic day that Washington faced down his officers in public meeting (diary, pp. 83–84). If the fate of the Republic was in the balance, Lieutenant Gilbert seems to have missed the excitement.

By March 1783, Benjamin Gilbert was in effect taking refuge in a disintegrating army—refuge from trouble awaiting at home in Brookfield, and refuge from the precarious uncertainties of life somewhere out on the post-Revolutionary American frontier. His accumulating promised pay as a serving officer, his credit (still good in local places of entertainment), the hospitality of neighboring civilians, the comradeship of fellow officers, the daily rations and shelter, and the status, however slight, conferred by his lieutenant's commission, as well as the honorable excuse for not facing Patience Converse and her father—all provided, despite his reiterated complaints of anxiety and boredom in the Army, a measure of security that Benjamin Gilbert seemed very reluctant to give up.

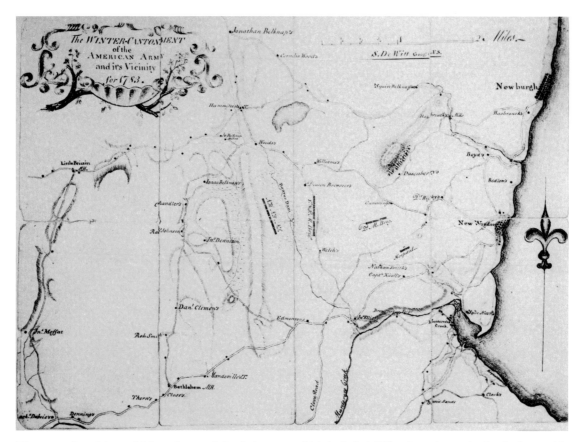

The camp site of the 2nd Massachusetts Brigade in 1783, which included Gilbert's regiment, is clearly discernible on this contemporary map by Simeon De Witt (by permission, from the original in The New-York Historical Society).

[30 September 1782]

Sir,

I received a letter the 24th Istant Signed John Cutler,[139] wrote at the request of yourself and Lady, the contents of which to me was very mortifying and foreign to my wishes. The misfortunes that have befel your Daughter and myself are Just punishments for our unwarrantable practises. But to have wounded the feelings of yourself, Lady and family, from whom I have received nothing but acts of kindness, and bring a Scandal on a family whom I always ought to venerate and Esteem (and I myself in part the cause) is a crime so capital that I am totally at a loss how to atone for. I shall leave service this fall, or the begining of the Ensuing Winter. Shall accelerate an opportunity of waiting on you to compromise the matter and do Justice to person and charactor of your Daughter, as an immediate matrimonial coalescence cannot extenuate our crimes nor a short crastination exaggerate them. I beg the matter may rest in its present State, till I Shall be enabled by my local Situation to settle the matter / if possible / to the Satisfaction of all parties. I am with every Sentiment of Esteem.

Yours etc.

30 September 82
Colonel James Converse

TO CAPTAIN JOHN CUTLER[140]

[30 September 1782]

Dear Sir

I received a letter from you bearing date September 8th 82 the contents of which caused in me great perturbations and perplexities of mind. But upon a mature deliberation I thought

138. The Converse family was prominent in Brook-field, as James' militia title would suggest. He was a selectman before the Revolution, and Gilbert, in his *Diary* for 13 February 1778 (p. 25), mentions seeing "Grandmother Converce." During his late-winter furloughs in 1780 and 1782, there are frequent references in the *Diary* to visits at the Converse household, increasingly abbreviated as "C.C." and sometimes suggesting that he stayed all night. We know from the unpublished diary that Gilbert was seeing Patience Converse during these visits. Her father James died in 1811, age 86. In addition to this letter and the following letter to John Cutler, Gilbert recorded in his diary for 30 September 1782 a letter written to "Miss Patience Converse." No letter to her, for any date, is in the letterbook.

139. See the letter below, and note.

140. The Cutlers were another prominent Brookfield family. John was married to Dorothy, the eldest daughter of Colonel Converse; he was also the older brother of Gilbert's comrade and correspondent, Isaac Cutler. John did not hold his rank in the Continental Army.

but to write my sentiments, which are inclosed, beg you to deliver them with your own hand. With my compliments to your Lady, I am

Superlatively yours etc.

30 September 82
Collaburgh[141]
Captain John Cuttler

TO HIS FATHER

[3 October 1782]

Honoured Sire

I received yours of the 11th Ultimo and was not a little surprised to here you had not received a letter from me in the course of the summer past. It must be owing to the neglect of those I entrusted the letters with. I have wrote a number of letters to you some to Mr. Joseph Dane and Mr. Charles Bruce. Have received no answers but from you and some of your numbers I have missed.

A Reduction of Regiments takes place throught the Army the first of January next.[142] The youngest[143] Officers of each grade and Regiment will be discharged. I being a young Lieutenant shall certainly leave Service. Shall be at home by the 12th of January next[144] if I can get money to bear my expences and a horse or Team to bring my Baggage. The Season is not less dry and destressing in this place than it is with you as mentioned in yours. The Inhabitents of the Country the greater half of them are Sick but the Army is healthy.

Compliments etc.

Collaburgh   3rd October 82
Captain Daniel Gilbert
No. 6

141. Croton Landing, NY.
142. This decision to create a smaller number of stronger regiments of at least 500 men by merging (thus eliminating some) regiments is fully described in the General Orders issued by Washington 30 October 1782, which includes the enabling act of the Continental Con-

gress. *Writings of Washington*, Fitzpatrick ed., xxv, pp. 310–13.

143. Most junior in seniority, not age.
144. In fact, Gilbert would not leave the army and return to Brookfield until November 1783.

[20 October 1782]

Honored Sire/

Since writing my last nothing has transpired worthy of notice. The Light Infantry remain Encamped near Croten River, the main Army at Verplanks Point. No arraingements for winter Quarters have been published. The Minister at war[145] has arived in Camp from Congress and is to proceed to the reduction of the Regiments immediately. The principal he proceeds on will certainly leave me out. I shall be at Brookfield the first of January next. Wish the Cloth for my Great Coat might be redy for makeing by that time as I shall be destitute of an over Coat.

The Financier being unable to furnish Mr. Sands the Contractor for the Army with any more money a Mr. Wadsworth has engaged to supply them on trust till the first of January next[146] Compliments etc.

Collaburgh   20th October 82

Captain Daniel Gilbert

No. 7

TO BRIGADIER GENERAL JOHN PATERSON[147]

[12 November 1782]

Sir

Your letter to the Officers of the Light Infantry requesting their sentiments on the arangement has been communicated. Mine are in favour of tarrying, and as my Number in the Grade of Lieutenant will Intitle me to a third in a company, I wish to be aranged accordingly.

I am

Sir etc.

November 12th 82

Brigadier General

Paterson

145. Secretary at War Benjamin Lincoln.

146. Comfort Sands (1748–1834) was a New York merchant and, with Alexander Hamilton, a future director of the Bank of New York. Jeremiah Wadsworth (1743–1804) was a Connecticut merchant who served as commissary to the French forces in America; he would later be president of the Bank of New York.

147. Commanding the 2nd Massachusetts Brigade, which included Gilbert's regiment. A Yale graduate (1762) and lawyer, Paterson later helped to organize the Ohio Company and to put down Shays' Rebellion in 1786. Gilbert's letter to Paterson suggests that he was not altogether candid in his earlier and later letters to his father and Colonel Converse, above and below, about leaving the army.

[16 November 1782]

Dear Sir

Had I any News foreign or domestick Should be Infinitely happy in transmitting it to you. The barren season for intelligence has put it wholly out of my power to furnish you with any. Had I been competent to the task should have attempted to have made some, but conscious of my own Inability I refer it to the more pregnant Witts.

My most sanguine expectations for some time past has been of quiting service this Winter. Some Resolves of Congress, and the pleasure of the Minister of War being Known, I find I cannot, consistent with a Millitary Character, Retire. As a Millitary calling is my present support, I think it more Eligable to persue it than to submit to a Political Death.

My present amusements consists chiefly in corrisponding with my friends, and in that I receive singular satisfaction, especially in yours as your letters are Replete with the sentiments of a Generous mind.

On the 26th Ultimo the main Army retired from their Camp at Verplanks and marched to the different places assined them for Hutting. The Massachusetts Line are at a place called Snake Hill west of New Windsor, the light Infantry remain in the field and are Encamped at the Continental Village[148] where we expect to continue till the first of January Next. Tomorrow the Company I belong to goes into the Jersies on Command. I expect our command will Short. Your favour of the 5th of October last has been Received. The interest you take in my preferment, and your felicitations there on, calls loudly for my acknowledgments.

Continental Village   November 16th 1782
Mr. Daniel Gould

TO HIS FATHER

[14 December 1782]

Honored Sir

Should this come to your hand before Ensign Potter[149] sets out for camp, wish you to send the cloth for my loose coat by him. Should he be set out on his Journy, or the cloth not finished, wish you to forward it by the first safe convayance.

148. Near Peekskill, on the east side of the Hudson.
149. Several Potters from Brookfield served in the war, but almost certainly this is Ephraim Potter, who had been enlisted for the Continental Army in 1777 by Gilbert's father out of Colonel Converse's militia regiment.

He was a sergeant by 1778 in the 5th Massachusetts Regiment, company sergeant-major by 1781, but is not listed in Massachusetts records as becoming an ensign, although an Ensign Potter (no first name) is listed in the 5th Massachusetts until he resigned in January 1783.

In my last I informed you I expected to leave service the first of January Next. Some Resolves of Congress and the pleasure of the Minister at War being known I find I cannot consistant with a military character leave service at present.

The Army has retired from the field, and are hutting back of New windsor. Their hutts are incomplete at present.

At my own request, I am transfered from the Light Infantry company to Captain Goodale's[150] which Company I have joined.

14th December 82
Captain Daniel Gilbert   New windsor
No. 8

TO HIS BROTHER-IN-LAW JOSEPH DANE

[17 December 1782]

Dear Sir

I have not been favoured with a line from you since I lift Brookfield. Whether it proceeds from neglect, or a miscarriage of letters, I shall not presume to determine, but shall be extreemly happy in receiving a letter from you should it contain nothing but the situation of yourself and Family.

I have not the least prospect of obtaining a Furlough this winter. Shall make myself as contented as possible in my present situatiaon. Neither Officer nor Soldier has received any money for the year 1782. No prospects of obtaining any soon.

Compliments etc.

New Windsor
December 17th 1782
Mr. Joseph Dane
No. 3

150. Nathan Goodale, born in Brookfield 1744, and a wartime hero. After the war, he joined the Ohio Company, was captured by hostile Indians in 1793, and died while being taken to British-held Detroit. Goodale figured importantly in Gilbert's abortive plans to settle after the war near Albany; see below.

[18 December 1782]

Honored Sir

The bearer of this, Lieutenant Smith,[151] will call on you. Beg you to use him as a Gentleman for my sake. He will apply to you for a note I consolidated when at Boston last winter, and one which you have consolidated since, if the interest on the last mentioned note is become due, if not he will not take it. He has directions from me to transact my business at Boston. Wish you to deliver the notes agreable to the above.

If Joseph Kimball has not taken my second and fourth Depreciation notes[152] to Boston wish you to deliver them to Lieutenant Smith takeing his receipt. On his return from Boston he will deliver the notes which he received from you, together with three notes more drawn in my favour, amounting to Eighteen pounds, Fourteen Shillings, and two pence each, which you will please to deposit with my other papers and give him a receipt for the same.

I wish you to continue to transact my matters as usual. If any part of my property can be disposed of by which money can be obtained without an injury to my interest, wish you to do it, and discharge my debts, perhaps the Note against Mr. Lomis may be paid, or some part of Mr. Ayre's.

Have you herd any thing from Reuben Gilbert. Have you received the sheep from Mr. Ranger. If you have how have you disposed of them. What success have you had in your manufatory of silk this year.

Are the people universally satisfyed with the new excise act, lately passed in your State.[153] How is Major harwood, has he got his Brick House built.[154] Reports have been spread in Camp that he is in low circumstances, which I am unwilling to believe.

How has the Law suit between Mr. Raymond and you terminated.

---

151. Of the dozens of Smiths serving from Massachusetts, Joseph, who was an officer in the 5th Massachusetts from 1777, lieutenant and quartermaster from 1778, and who served until June 1783, fits the role assigned to him in Gilbert's correspondence, and is positively identified in Gilbert's diary on 22 March 1783.

152. As the name suggests, these were supplements issued by the State to make up for losses caused by inflation in the promised but unpaid salaries owed to officers and men. Ferguson, *Power of the Purse*, pp. 50–51, explains that these depreciation certificates would comprise a great part of the State war debts, whose "assumption" by the Federal government would become a crucial and highly controversial feature of the policies pursued by Secretary of the Treasury Alexander Hamilton.

153. Direct State taxes on wine, tea, rum, brandy, and carriages. Van Beck Hall, *Politics Without Parties: Massachusetts, 1780–1791* (Pittsburgh, 1972), pp. 111–21, answers Gilbert's question to his father; in brief, the new taxes both aroused opposition and were inadequate to the fiscal needs of the State.

154. Major Peter Harwood's house was as late as 1798 the only brick house in Brookfield. According to the town's historian, building it bankrupted him and caused him to leave town. Temple, *Brookfield*, pp. 267, 617–18. He was a millwright, whose father had died at Louisbourg in King George's War, and had been Gilbert's company commander in the campaigns of 1775–76.

You Kneed not look for me home this winter. Captain Goodale and Lieutenant Smith claim a prior wright to a Furlough. General Orders forbid but one Officer from a Company to be absent at a time.

Complimemts etc.

Camp New Windsor
December 18th 1782   No. 9
Captain Daniel Gilbert

Directions given Lieutenant [Joseph] Smith   December 19 [1783]

Sir

You will please to call on my father in your way to Boston and receive from him a Note of Eleven pounds and upwards, which Mr. Flagg got consolidated for me last winter, and one which my father consolidated since, if the Interest on the last mentioned note is become due. If my father has not sent my second and fourth Deprecaition notes to Boston, wish you to take them and get them Consolidated. When at Boston you will make application for the Interest due on my notes, and if so fortunate as to obtain the payment of it, you will please to dispose of the money in the following maner. /Viz/ purchase one silver appalet, lining for two Shirts. If any money remains bring it on to Camp. On your return you will call on my father, deliver him all the notes which you have of mine, taking his receipt for the same. Wish you to inquire of my father when returning, whether he has sent the cloth for my loose Coat, If not, and you should be a horseback, wish you to bring it with you.

TO HIS FATHER

[19 December 1782]

Honored Sir

Since writing No. 9, I received your favour of December 10 No. 12. I find by that, you have received my sheep of Mr. Ranger, that part of them are bespoak. If Mr. Taylor will take them on the same principal that they have been let heretofore, I wish he may have as many as he chuses, provided his circumstances are good, of which you are a proper Judg. What remains I wish you to sell, if they bear a good price, and discharge a Note Lieutenant Colonel Newhall has against me. If any money remains call on Mr. Joseph Dane, who has two Notes against me, and satisfy him as far as the money will go. I am not a little surprised to find your last letter No. 12 when I have received but five, the first bears Date May 11th, no number, another June 1st No. 2, one June 25th No. 4, and one September 11th without a number. No. 12 I this moment received by the hand of Thaddeaus Potter.[155] If any matters of importance were committed to the deficient numbers wish you to repeat them in your next.

No. 10
December 19th 82
Captain Daniel Gilbert

TO HIS STEPBROTHER AARON KIMBALL

[31 December 1782]

Dear Sir

I am sorry to be under the disagreable necessaty of taxing you with a breach of friendship, but your conduct is so apparant it will not bear a milder construction. Our interchangable promisses were such at the time of our parting, that I considered myself under the greatest obligations, to embrace every opportunity presenting in writing to you, and doubted not but you would be as chearfull in answering, but I have been grosely deceived, and instead of mutual corrispond my time has been spent in writing not reading. For some time I flattered myself, your Justification would arise from a want of conveyance, but the time has so far elapsed that I find no excuse for you, and must attribute your silence to prepence[156] neglect.

I should be happy could you prevail with yourself to write one line, and Justify yourself or desire me to cease writing.

I have wrote in the plain familiar stile of friendship without reserve, which is a language I always wish to be addressed, and which I hope will not be offencive to him who I take the pleasure of subscribing myself. Dear Sir etc.

B Gilbert

New Windsor   December 31st 82
Mr. Aaron Kimball

155. Thaddeus Potter was a Brookfield boy, but apparently not a soldier in 1782. In 1778, he had served briefly as a 14-year-old volunteer for a few months to guard the British and Hessian prisoners from Burgoyne's army. After the war he moved to South Hadley, then to Vermont, where he died in 1833.

156. Premeditated. The angry tone of this letter may be explained by the letter that follows, in which Gilbert thanked Charles Bruce for sending news of the Converse affair but blamed other friends for not keeping him informed.

[30 December 1782]

Dear Sir

By the mouth of Thaddeus Potter I received some information and advice from you, which I return you my cincere thanks for. They were matters I was totally a stranger to. No-one of my friends haveing been so polite as to advertise me of what had transpired since I left Brookfield, all the information I had received on the subject alluded to above, was from common fame which very much varied in its reports. I doubt not you and every segacious person will (when you seriously consider the officious conduct of Captain J. C.) conclude that he was particularly interested, and backed by one If Justice was to take place, would be the only person called in question.[157] I shall not deliver my sentiments in so minute a manner as I should do provided I [k]new the Issue of the matter, but wish you to write me by the first saft conveyance giving a full detail of all circumstances, their events, and reports as they are propagated by the Vulgar, pointing out those characters who have made themselves most buisy in aspersing my charater that I may know who are friend, and who are foes.

Compliments etc.

December 30th 82
Mr. Charles Bruce

TO HIS FATHER

New Windsor January 11th [17]83

Honored Sir/

I am unwilling to put you to any trouble either in body or mind, but my present necessaties obliges me to do it. I would therefore request you to exert your utmost to obtain the payment of some of the private securities which you have in your posession belonging to me. If that is impractacable, I wish you to hire 30 or 40 pounds of cash for me. If you cannot obtain it at simple interest, I would rather have you give 20 per cent Interest than not get it. The money I shall want by the first of March Next, at which time I shall draw an order on you for that sum

---

157. The rank of captain makes it clear that by "J.C." Gilbert refers not to Colonel James Converse, the father of the pregnant Patience, but to John Cutler, the husband of her sister Dorothy, and the agent of the Converse family in dealing with Gilbert (letters of 30 September 1782, above). The other "person" referred to in the letter, the probable culprit who allegedly made John Cutler an interested party in the affair, may have been his brother Isaac, who had accompanied Gilbert on at least one of his nocturnal visits to the Converse household (*Diary*, p. 75, 13 March 1782). By the time of this letter to Bruce, Patience Converse must have been very near the term of her pregnancy.

and if it is not in your power to discharge the order, I shall be under the disagreable Necessaty of selling the greater part of my state securities at 5 or 6 shillings per pound, which is a mesure I am unwilling to pursue. However I would not have you put yourself to any considerable expence or trouble on the matter for I would rather chuse to sell the whole of my securities at a great discount, than put you under any great embarresment.

I received your favour by the hand of Ensign Potter, together with cloth and thread for a loose Coat. I cannot find words to express my Gratitude on the occasion. It was a seasionable relief and merrits my warmest thanks. Peace is much talked of and it is the prevailing opinion that it take place in the spring. The Army is in a healthy state, and well supplyed with provisions.

Compliments etc.

January 11th 1783
Captain D. Gilbert   No. 11

New windsor, January 18th [17]83

Dear Sisters

Chastity is a Virtue worthy the pursute of every noble mind, that it is pursued by the female world in general no one can pretend to aver.

Mr alliworthy to Jenny Jones[159]

Gallantry and amoures intrigues has become so prevalent, (with sorrow I aver it) a great part of your sex are deceived and debauched thereby.

If the above advice and arguments against such deception, appear to be founded on the bassis of reason, I wish you to have recourse to them when ever you find yourself in danger of being overpowered.

I am Dear sisters
with every sentiment of Affection
and Esteem (and who has your welfare nearest his heart
your loving brother B Gilbert

Miss Esther and Mary Gilbert

---

158. Esther was age 20 when this letter was written, Mary 17.
159. These exact words could not be found in Squire

Allworthy's admonitions to Jenny Jones in Henry Fielding's *The History of Tom Jones*, published in 1749.

New Windsor   January 11th 1783

Dear Sir

I doubt not but you will immediately on receipt of this, have recourse to the signature, and when you find my name subscribed, draw a conclusion from my professional capacity, that the subject is worthy your perusal but alas! How will your indignation rise, when you find the deception, a Rhapsody, a Vacum, substituted for common sence. But my dear sir, I should not have troubled you, in this manner, had it not been for the interchangable promises between us, to continue our corrispond, in improveing every opportunity of writing, had I neglected the present, you might construed it to prepence neglect.

I flatter myself you will acknowledg the continuation of my corrispondence in a litteral sence, tho not in a real one. A conscientiousness that this would shew the goodness of my intentions, I thought it more eligable to discover the barreness of my Ideas, and my inability of performing to your expectations, than to subject mysilf to your Censure.

Mr. Daniel Gould

TO HIS FATHER

January 18, 1783

Honored Sir

In my last, I pressed you to furnish me with a sum of money, (without giving you any account what use I should put it too).

I now inform you that there is a tract of Land in the county of Albany, which will be confiscated, in March next.[160] The land is of a quality equil to any on the continent. It may be purchased by way of Location at a much cheaper rate than at private sale. Captain Goodale and others, will deal largely in that way, and are anxious to have me become a partner with them. I am convinced it will add greatly to our interest if we persue this measure, although my finances are small I would wish to venture a part or all of it. Captain Goodale who transmits this can inform you of every particular relative to the matter, and has an order on you for the money I wrote for in my last. He will inform you at what time he shall sett out for camp. If it is possible to procure the sum I wrote for, or only a part, I wish you to deliver it to him. If it is not, you will please to deliver him as many of my securities, as he shall be disposed to receive, takeing his receipt for the same.

160. The large number of Loyalist supporters of Britain in New York made the punitive confiscation of their lands a major aspect of the Revolution in that State.

Colonel Putnam is promoted to a Brigadier General, and is annexed to the third Brigade,[161] which he has taken command of. He presents his compliments to you through me. I wish you to send some white woolen yarn (to mend Stockings with) by Lieutenant Smith when he returns to camp. I should not have made this application if I could purchase any in this place.

Compliments etc.

No. 12
Captain D Gilbert

TO HIS FATHER

[30 January 1783]

Ever Dear Reverend and Honored Sir

I received your favour of the 18th of January last, with the supplement inclosed, by the hand of corporal Kimball.[162] It is with infinite pleasure I perceive your readiness therein to espouse my cause in endeavouring to procure the money I wrote for.

If it is not obtained either by payment or hire, I shall impute it to the hardness of the times, and my Illfortune. The cloth you sent me by the hand of Ensign Potter proves to be a full pattern, and is superior in quality to my expectations. I thank you for complying with my request of the 18th December last, and doubt not every requisition of mine founded on reason, and in your power of complying with, will be readily fulfilled.

The Supplement inclosed in yours of the 18th Instant contains matter worthy of serious consideration and will sensibly touch the feelings of every breast impressed with a delicate sensation. It is a matter that ought to affect all, as it respects mankind in general, and should not be treated lightly by any. That I as an individual am obligated conscientiously to regard it any further than its fame (as propagated by the Vulgar) is a matter cannot fully be assertained by the populace. Your first information you say was from Doctor Kitterage,[163] that it was then conjectured by some persons Captain Cutler was the guilty person (I am more surprised at the credulity of those who have made themselves busy than at any event that hath taken place). If

161. The 5th Massachusetts, Gilbert's regiment, was in the 2nd Brigade.

162. Corporal Kimball was almost certainly Gilbert's stepbrother Joseph Kimball of Brookfield, who had been enlisted at age 21 for three years out of Captain Daniel Gilbert's Company of Colonel Rice's Regiment of militia in January 1781, promoted corporal in the 4th Massachusetts Regiment, and would serve in the West Point garrison until November 1783. Like his brother Aaron, Joseph Kimball shared with Benjamin Gilbert a

stepmother, Mary, the second wife and widow of Benjamin Kimball and the third wife of Daniel Gilbert

163. Jacob Kittridge came from a Brookfield family of doctors without college degrees, and is described by the town historian as a "far-famed surgeon" to whom all came for relief. With Gilbert's father Daniel, Dr. Kittridge led the successful fight in 1810–11 to make the second or north precinct of Brookfield the separate town of North Brookfield. He died in 1813. Temple, *Brookfield*, pp. 260–65, 268, 291, 664–65.

they had had common sagacity or once recollected that he had a brother,[164] that frequented being in company with Miss, not only when she was at Captain Cutlers, but at her fathers, and that unless some briberey was made use of to turn her allegation Captain Cutlers Brother should be called in question, they could not be at a loss how to account for Captain Cutlers officious conduct.

Scandal is such a prevalent evil in Brookfield, that while I have so many enemies in that place who wish to destroy my charactor, Interest, and Life, could they take it without being called to an account, that no friend of mine need be at a loss from whence all of this clamour proceeds. I pity the poor Girl, to think she should be deluded and flattered into a notion, that if she acquited the father of the child,[165] and called on an innocent person, she should be the gainer. Common fame declares this to be fact.

But I have this consolation, my conscience informs me I stand acquited by my God
This self evident Vindication over swells and bears down all the clamor of the Vulgar.

Another consideration arises that is founded on a true maxim, which is, while a person remains in obscurity slander touches him not. But as soon as his person or charater becomes conspicuous, Stigma, Scandal, and every Epithet, or appellation, that their own invention can produce, or the inspiration of the muses assisted by Alecto, minos and all Infernal furies can dictate, is immediately applyed. There is no one General Rule which has so few exceptions as this—that where the aspersions of the peasantry is universal, the Character is eminent. I could say much more on the subject, but I think the foregoing hints are sufficient to give you an idea on what basis all this Clamor is founded, and from what source it springs. I beg you and every friend of mine to suspend your Judgments untill you shall se me, at which time you will be informed of many matters which will corroborate with the above, and acquit me as fully as I now appear guilty to the world.

The mild and complacent manner in which you have treated the subject in your supple-memt is a specemin of your goodness, and calls for my most serious acknowledgments. No reflections arises from the before recited matter, that causes in me such unpleasing sensations as thoughts of the disagreeable contemplations It will cause in the minds of my dear parents and friends, while it stands in its present light. I have made use of many invectives in the course of my disertation, which is not meant for your community at large, but only for those excreable miscreants, who have made scurrility their Topical head of discourse, but as I am independant of their favours, I despise their satirial sarcasms, and shall take no more notice of, or consider it of any more consequence than the en[v]y of a Mob. As the subject is disagreable I here close

164. This is an unmistakable reference to Isaac Cutler, Gilbert's comrade and correspondent.

165. This is the only evidence in Gilbert's letters and diary that a child was actually born.

it. That we shall soon have a peace I think is an incontestable supposition. When that happy event takes place, I hope to have the supreme Filicity of visiting my relations and friends. Till then I remain Honored Sire with every sentiment of filial Duty yours etc.　　B Gilbert

New Windsor 30th January 1783　　As you propose to begin your numbers with the year, I follow your Example, and having wrote two before this, I number this 3.
Captain Gilbert

TO CAPTAIN NATHAN GOODALE

[31 January 1783]

Dear Captain,

Captain Bowmans tryal is published and his punishments amounts to this, to beg Colonel Newhalls pardon, in presence of the Brigade, and suffer three months suspention.[166] Captain Bowman is unwell and remains in the Country. Colonel Newhall is not arrested, nor will he be till your return. You being a principal evidence, the Captain is unwilling to have the tryal commence without your being present, as it would if the Colonel was now put in arrest.[167]

Colonel Brooks[168] is returning from Congress, and is bringing some proposals for the consideration of the Army. There is a prospects of the Armies receiving one Months pay soon, which will be in Morrisses Bills[169] payable in thirty Days from their dates. No money has come into the pay Office sinc you lift this place.

January 31st 83　　Captain Goodale

TO RUFUS HAMILTON

[31 January 1783]

Dear Sir

I this Day had the supreme Filicity of hearing the peck of Corn you gave Mr. Pope, has

166. Captain Phineas Bowman, probably of Brook-field, was tried by a general court-martial in January 1782 for conduct unbecoming an officer and gentleman toward his commanding officer (i.e., Colonel Ezra New-hall); the verdict and sentence were as reported by Gilbert (*Writings of Washington*, Fitzpatrick ed., XXVI, p. 49).

167. It appears that Captain Bowman had lodged some kind of counter-charge against Newhall, but neither a trial nor an offense is mentioned in the published Washington papers, although Massachusetts records indicate that Newhall was under arrest briefly in May 1783.

168. Colonel John Brooks (1752–1825) of Medford, MA, who had represented army grievances both to the State government in Boston and to the Continental Congress. His role, if any, in the subsequent "Newburgh conspiracy" remains unclear.

169. Notes signed by Robert Morris, the Superintendent of Finance, and issued in denominations from $20 to $100. As usual, Ferguson, *Power of the Purse*, is highly informative and clear on the subject, pp. 136–39, 164, 169–74.

had the desired effect and that he or some supernatural power, had given you a son and heir.[170] I sincerely congratulate you on the happy event, and give you and your lady Joy.

I am informed that some people have taken their Daughters to Mr. pope, and that their success has been equil to yours, whether corn is plenty or they admire the Breed I cannot determine, but I think it will not cause so much Joy.[171] I am etc.

N Windsor   31 January 83
Mr. Rufus Hamilton

TO HIS FATHER

[6 March 1783]

Honored Sir

I received your favor of the 16th of February last by the hand of Lieutenant Smith. Although you have but little prospects of getting money for me, I am perfectly satisfyed as to your exertions on the occation, and am fully perswaded was it in your power to procure it, I should have it whether from Debtors or hire. I have been informed that Mr. Reuben Gilbert has been in Brookfield this winter. I wish to know whether he called on you. If he did, what encoragements he gave relative to a settlement.

I have the happyness of informing you that the soldiers this Day received half a Crown[172] per Man. The payment is to continue weekly in the same proportion for thirteen weeks successively. The Officers get no pay as yet, and very little prospects of getting any at any period.

If you should get any money for me after Captain Goodale leaves Brookfield wish you not to send it unless you are sure that it will have a saft conveyance.

BG

N Windsor   6th March 1783[173]   No. 4
Captain Gilbert

170. Isaac Hamilton, born 12 January 1783, son of Rufus and Polley, died 29 August 1784.

171. Reference in this letter is obviously to some kind of early American fertility ritual, perhaps described in the missing letter from Hamilton to Gilbert. Mr. Pope has not been identified.

172. Two shillings, six pence, or about 70 cents at then current rates. Ferguson, *Power of the Purse*, p. 164, says that Morris had begun to pay the soldiers at the rate of 50 cents per month. See Gilbert's letter to Captain Jonathan Stone, 1 March 1783, below, for what appears to be a more accurate version of how Morris was paying the Army.

173. Why this letter is a month out of date order (between letters dated 31 January and 3 February) is not clear; perhaps Gilbert had inadvertently skipped a sheet, and later used it for this letter. He wrote in the month as "March" after scratching out "February."

[3 February 1783]

Dear Sir

Your favour of the 23d January this day came saft to hand, the contents of which caused in me an alternate succession of the contrasted passion of sorrow, and Joy. With sorrow I read the account of your late unfortunate sickness, and my impatience to know the issue, scarcely gave me time to observe what time happened. But oh! how quick was that disagreeable feeling banished from my breast, when in the succeeding lines I found that you not only had arived to, but still was in, good Health. Then my anxiety immediately subsided, and Joy calmly seated itself in my breast. The frigorific[174] season and multiplicity of business, prevents me from expatiating on the above or any other subject.

Shall just inform you that we have the most sanguine expectations of Peace in the spring, and have very many corroborating circumstances. Should such a happy event take place, I shall expect the supreme filicity of conversing with you face, to face. Till then you may rest assured my friendship is sincere, and that it is placed on a worthy object is the Opponion of

Dear Sir

with Every sentiment of
Esteem your Obedient Humble Servant
BGilbert

N Windsor   3 February 1783
Mr. D Gould Western

TO LIEUTENANT [DANIEL?] OGDEN[175]

[16 February 1783]

Dear Sir

I this Day had the supreme Filicity of receiving a Letter from you. Nothing could have made an addition to that happyness, but the pleasure of seing you. I thank you for writing. Had time and opportunity admitted of giving me a Detail of your proceedings, since I had the pleasure of seing you, I should have read it with infinite satisfaction. I presume your desire to se me will not be put of[f] at a Distant period, for we have the most sanguine expectations of a speedy Peace, and every Circumstance corroborates with our expectations. Should that happy event take place, the Troops of the different Line will be Marched to their own States before

---

174. In the dictionary, believe it or not, defined as causing cold.

175. On Lieutenant Ogden, see previous letter from Gilbert of 20 May 1782 and note, above.

they are disbanded.[176] Ours will undoubtedly march through Springfield. I shall then do myself the pleasure of calling on you, and give you a relation of many matters, which would be too Vollumnious to commit to this paper. In the mean time I beg you to continue your corrispondance, and I assure you not one of your letters shall pass unnoticed by your

Sincere friend and Humble
Servant

February 16th 1783

BGilbert

Lieutenant Ogden Springfield

TO CAPTAIN JONATHAN STONE[177]

[1 March 1783]

Dear Sir

I thank you for your favour of the 22d Ultimo. I should be happy to give you any agreable information from our quarter, was it in my power, but as it is not, please to accept such as you shall find in the sequel of this letter.

Captain Trotter[178] who has acted in the Capacity of A.D.C. [aide-de-camp] to Brigadier General Putnam for some time past, having been sufficiently Chaargrined by many of his grade, for leaving the *Honorary* Command of a Company for that of A.D.C. to a B.G. has almost prevailed with himself to resume the Command of a Company. Captain Benson[179] Commands the Light [Infantry] Company. Major Ashley[180] is Transfered to the 6th Massachusetts Regiment and Major [Moses] Knap[181] to the 5th Regiment. They Join accordingly this Day.

---

176. Gilbert was wrong in this prediction; the troops of the Continental line were simply disbanded in and around West Point; see his letter, below, of 10 June 1783 to Charles Bruce.

177. Previously identified as the commander of the company of light infantry in which Gilbert served, Captain Jonathan Stone became a staunch Federalist, like Gilbert, after the war. He joined the Society of the Cincinnati, and in 1786 was active in putting down Shays' Rebellion, in which his elder brother Francis, also a wartime captain, played a leading role. Their father had been killed in the taking of Quebec in 1759, and left his sons the family tannery. Jonathan married a niece of General Rufus Putnam and died 1801 in Ohio. Francis,

after fleeing to Vermont, received a pardon, and returned to Brookfield, but never expressed any regret for his part in the 1786 rebellion. Temple, *Brookfield*, p. 748. *Memorials of the Massachusetts Society of the Cincinnati*, ed. Frank Smith (Boston, 1931), p. 437.

178. Captain John Trotter, who appears to have been from Brookfield, would serve as aide to General Rufus Putnam to the end of the war.

179. Captain Joshua Benson served from 1775 to the end of the war.

180. See Gilbert's previous letter to Captain Moses Ashley 1 June 1781, above, and note.

181. Major Moses Knapp had risen from sergeant in 1775 and would serve until June 1783; he died in 1809.

The Officers of the Army (except those who served in Virginia in 1781)[182] will immediately draw Notes for one Months pay, payable in two Months from the date. The Soldiers will receive half a Dollar per week in cash untill the sum amounts to 40/[183] We have the most sanguine expectations of a speedy Peace. All News form Europe corrobborates with our expectations.

I am extreemly happy to find my arrangements for Domestick Life meets with your approbation, and what adds to my filicity is you appearing to favour and partake of the same.

I had entered into some Negotiation on the matter, which I had great prospects of carrying on with sucess, but this rumor and bustle about a peace has wholly frustrated my design.[184] This disappointment causes me to prick a New. However, I expect immediately, after the arrival of Captain Goodale in Camp, we shall be able to procure such papers as shall secure us those Lands we have in contemplation.

I am under the disagreable Necessaty of informing you that I have not been acquainted with any new Gods except some auxilars to the unfortunate ones. Divils I could give you a large detail of but as you have plenty, I will not presume to Trouble you with any more.

Now for Congress. They have been pleased to resolve that they will niether settle nor commute with us, nor recommend it to our states.[185] In addition to their good Offices they have resolved that they will not allow any settlement made by the different States, no later than the first of August 1780. Consequently our securities for nine months pay of 1780 must be subject to a discount of 5/9 both principal and Interest whenever presented for payment. A part of the Committe have returned from Congress, the others are expected soon.[186]

We have established a Seraglio[187] at a place Vulgalarly called Wyoma where we have super

182. Why officers who had served in the Yorktown campaign of 1781 were excepted is not clear; Joseph Clay of Georgia, deputy paymaster-general for the southern armies, had resigned; as an appointee of Congress, his accounts had to be settled by the Treasury, which may explain the exception and consequent delay. *The Papers of Robert Morris*, vi, p. 611.

183. A little less than $10 at then current rates.

184. His meaning is clearer in the letter to his father of 18 January 1783, above, where he identifies the land he hopes to acquire in Albany County, NY, as scheduled for confiscation as Loyalist property by the State in March 1783. The peace treaty negotiated at Paris specifically forbade any further such confiscation.

185. Army accounts were hung up in Congress on the political and constitutional question of a general fund under Congressional control. Eventually, under pressure from Washington, Congress commuted the promised pension to officers into five years' full pay, paid in the form of federal securities. Ferguson, *Power of the Purse*, p. 164.

186. The return of this delegation from Philadelphia and its disappointing report on the Congressional response to Army grievances led directly to the controversial "Newburgh conspiracy," which Washington managed to quash. For the continuing debate among scholars about what actually happened at Newburgh in mid-March, see the articles by Richard H. Kohn and Paul David Nelson in *The William and Mary Quarterly*, 3rd ser. xxvii, pp. 187–220, and xxix, pp. 143–58. Gilbert himself was either oblivious to these events or failed to record them in his diary or letterbook.

187. Clearly Gilbert refers to a brothel or its equivalent. Professor Ira Gruber of Rice University tells me that the word is frequently used in this sense by British officers in the 18th century.

fine Kippen Issued immediately on application. We draw on seperate orders, I make my returns once a week and receive a full ration without giving a receipt for the same.[188]

We have established a New Corps in the 5th [Massachusetts]. They have the title of Helion. Lieutenant Warren is appointed to the Right Wing, Ensign Wing to the Left, Lieutenant P. Holland to the Staff, they do duty in rotation. The particulars of their duty is as follows (Viz) reconnoitre all Seraglios, Inspect into their Police, Invent lies for the Day and propogate them, make report of all Kippen Issued, and where the best Stores are and many minutiae too Tedious to mention.

my compliments to your
Lady father and Mother

I am Dear Sir
        with every
Sentiment of Esteem
Your Obedient Humble Servant
B Gilbert

N.B. Colonel Newhall
is transferred to
the 4th M[assachusetts]R[egiment].
Lieutenant Smith Compliments
to you

Cantonment N. Windsor
March 1st 1783
Captain J. Stone

188. Soldier slang for prostitutes or available women. The etymology is obscure. In vulgar English, a kip can mean a nap, and a kip-house a low lodging house, even a brothel. There seems little doubt that "Wyoma" was a brothel or group of brothels somewhere near the town of Newburgh and the New Windsor encampment, north of West Point. According to his diary, on Thursday, 20 February 1783, about a week before this letter to Stone, Gilbert and two friends first visited "Wyoma," where they "spent a very agreable Night," returning to camp at sunrise next day. Subsequently, Gilbert recorded no less than fifteen visits to "Wyoma," often on Sunday, usually with Dr. James Edwards Burr Finley, surgeon of the 5th Massachusetts Regiment and son of the fifth president of the College of New Jersey (modern Princeton University), and Ensign Jonathan Wing of the 5th Regiment. Gilbert made his last visit to "Wyoma," with Wing, on Thursday, 20 June 1783, when they "drank Tea with the Girls, & staid all night." A few days later, the Massachusetts Regiments were ordered to march to Philadelphia to suppress the mutiny of the Pennsylvania Line. After returning to West Point, Gilbert received on 26 August "a disagreable letter from Wy[oma]." Given his difficult economic circumstances during the winter and spring of 1783, and the fact that he had received part of his pay on 29 July, the letter from "Wyoma," which surely extended credit to frequent but impecunious guests like Gilbert, may have been a dunning note.

[6 March 1783]

Dear Sir/

Nothing could equil my happiness on receiving your favour of the 22d of February last. I think myself under the greatest obligation to you, for the trouble you have given yourself on my account, in endeavouring to procure every information possible relative to my character and Interest. The Complicated reports that prevail amongst you give me very little uneasiness, tho I thank you for giving a detail of them. Facts are the only things that will influence my conduct. You gave a hint about a letter said to be wrote by me,[189] and say that she expects that I will marry her. In answer to that, I declare that if no man is more guilty than myself, she has conceived without the seed of man. And that she never had any of mine is a truth she cannot deny. From the above declaration, and your knowledge of my principalls and disposition, I leave you to Judge what grounds she has to found her hopes on.

But in answer to the more agreable part of your letter, I must acknowledge, the compliments of a young Lady, for whom I have utmost veneration and esteem, was so pleasing, that the thoughts of my misfortune, was wholly absorbed in that agreable reflection, I should have had the presumption to have wrote to her, had I not been well assured after what had past between us that she would have considered it as impertinent and an intrusion on her domestick happiness. And what adds to my misfortune is this, altho she has parted with her pomfret Gentleman[190] I dare not presume to hope (this I say to you in confidence). I beg the favour, that the first opportunity presenting you make my compliments in the most respectful manner to her.

Compliments etc.

BG

March 6th 1783   No. 3

Mr. Charles Bruce

---

189. This seems to refer to Gilbert's letter to Colonel James Converse of 30 September 1782, above, in which he virtually admitted that he must have been the father of Colonel Converse's daughter's unborn child. Without the reference here, and in light of Gilbert's subsequent denial of paternity, one might plausibly conclude that Gilbert, after drafting the 30 September letter in his letterbook, had never actually sent it.

190. Not identified, nor is the woman in question known.

New Windsor 6th March 1783

Dear Sir

I received a Letter from Brookfield a few Days since, the supplement of which informed me that [you] were in a few Days to quit the regions of Liberty, and inclose yourself in the indelable Bands of Matrimony with a Miss Butler, A Lady of Celebrated Beauty and distinguished merrit. I congratulate you on your approaching filicity. I hope the Nuptial Torch, will give light and Joy to the succeeding part of your Days. Although crosses, misfortunes, and disappointments are the partners of my Lot, yet I rejoice in the good fortune of my friends, and in no ones more than yours.

The Gentlemen of the Army remain in statequo as to their pay, but the mode of victualing them is quite altered since I saw you, and is much for the better.

Doctor Bartlet   I am etc.   B Gilbert

TO HIS COUSIN DANIEL GOULD

[12 March 1783]

Dear Sir/

Times or'e swelling waves has at length wasted away another winter, and the season is approaching when Pheobus's periodical visits to this part of Earth appears most enlivening. Although Nature will soon be in her Bloom and the feathered Choir will be hovering around us, warbling in their Throats their Melodias songs Vying with [one an]other, which shall most enchant our Ears, or Engage our attention, yet one thing is wanting to complete our Temporal Happiness.

Peace thou Darling Attribute of the Gods, and sole comforter of the humane species, who has not deigned to Visit this Continent for near Eight years, 'tis she we wish to come and take up her Abode with us. If this wished for blessing should arrive with Natures bloom, I should share a Double portion of its favours. I should not only partake of the general Joy which will infuse itself among Mankind, but have the supreme Filicity of seeing my friend again, which

---

191. Dr. John Bartlett of Rhode Island was Physician and Surgeon-General in the Northern Department of the Continental Army from 1777, and may have been the man who cared for Gilbert during his illness of 1778–79. Frequent references to Dr. Bartlett in the *Diary* indicate that he lived in or near Brookfield, and was a close friend of the Gilbert family. Vital records indicate that he was a half-brother of Azubah Bartlett; see letter to her of [December 1780], above.

will be the summit of my ambition, both of which I have the most sanguine expectation of enjoying before the revolution of many Months. Untill that happy period, I wish the continuence of your Correspondence.

I have no new to Transmit you worthy your attention, or I should not have prefaced my Letter with such a Rhapsody, void of Analogy or Syntax, but as it [is] from a sincere friend, I hope you will pardon it. It is a maxim held truly sacred, by an antient Philosopher, that it is more Eligable to conceal or pass over the faults of a friend, than to expose his weekness to the world. With full confidence that you will not be less humane than the antient Heathens, I send you this as a token of my sincerity and weakness.

and am etc.   BG

12 March 83
Mr. D Gould

TO HIS FATHER

New Windsor   17 March 1783

Honored Sir

I received your favour by the hand of Captain Goodale, with the money mentioned theirin. I was not a little surprised to find you had mistook my meaning in No. 12 bearing date January 18th. If [you] peruse it you will find a clause to this purpose (Viz) you will please to deliver him (meaning Captain Goodale) as ma[n]y of my securities, as he shall be disposed to recive, takeing his receipt for the same. Those securiities I did expect him to sell for Cash and bring it on to me, to enable me to become an adventurer with him in Locating Lands. This unfortunate mistake has put it wholly out of my power to prosecute any business of that kind unless something can be done speedily. I request you to take the 48 pound note consolidated by Lieutenant Smith and carry it to old Mr. Partrick of Werston, who has cash by him, and is anxious to lay it out in state securities. He pressed Captain Goodale to let him have a large sum for eight shillings on the pound. If he will take that note and pay you the Cash in hand or one half down and other in three weeks wish you to let him have it. Try for Nine shillings but [do not?] fall lower than 7/. which is the current price in Boston. If you cannot trade with Mr. Partrick nor no one in the Town, please to deliver it to Mr. David Hitchcok, and request him to send it to Boston by Mr. Hide the post, and let him get what the Current price is in Boston. The money arising from my Note or any other money that you may collect for me between this and the Tenth of April, if you leave it with Captain Lincoln you may depend on its meeting with a saft conveyance by Doctor Lawton of our Regiment who will call on Captain Lincoln on his way to Camp. If you should not obtain any money for me before the 10 of Aprill, and

[90]

should get any afterwards deliver it to Mr. David Hitchcok who has money to send on to Captain Goodale, and it will meet with a saft conveyance. Wish you to take a receipt for all money or Notes you may leave with in trust with any person for me or on my account.

The approaching Peace makes it requisit that I make some arrangements for domestick Life. Should I neglect that, or fail in my attempt, I should be as miserable, as I have been endeavouring, this Eight years, to make my Country happy.[192]

My Compliments to the

Family

I am Honored Sir etc.

B Gilbert

Captain Gilbert
No. 5

TO COLONEL JAMES CONVERSE

New Windsor   24th March 1783

Sir

I acknowledge the Receipt of yours of the 1st of March, the contents I cooley, and deliberately considered, and the subject I have perfectly discussed some time since. But I cannot at present follow your advice without relinquishing every Idea of Honor, (which I hold much dearer than life) and destroy my interest, and every expectation of reward for past services, which is a measure I am sure no friend of mine can wish me to adopt. It would be too Volluminous to give you an extract of all General Orders Issued relative to Officers, or soldiers, quiting the field, at the present important Crisis. Let this Suffice, I cannot obtain leave of absence, nor at present comply with your request without quiting every Idea of future Temporal Happiness, and makeing my myself as miserable as I have this Eight years endeavoured to make my Country Happy.

You may rest assured that I shall make it the first object of my persute after I arive in Brookfield, to compromise the matter with yourself and Family, which period cannot be supposed to be at a great distance, as every account from Europe confirms what we have for some time past been advertised of.

192. One of the disappointments of the letterbook and the diary is Gilbert's failure to describe or even mention the "Newburgh" affair, on 15 March 1783, when Washington confronted and quashed an officers' plot to coerce Congress into providing for the Army.

I expected my letters to yourself and Daughter bearing Date 22d December 1782[193] would have sufficiently satisfyed you on the subject, and convinced you that I as a military Man who considers nothing relative to this life so binding as my Honor that (when ever Circumstances would admit), nothing should be wanting on my part to do your Daughter that Justice which she has a right to expect from me.

> My Compliments to your Lady
> Daughter and Family I am Sir

Colonel J. Converse

TO HIS BROTHER-IN-LAW CHARLES BRUCE

New Windsor 25th March 1783

Dear Sir

Since my last, I have received a letter from Colonel Converse, in which he gives it as has oponion, that It would be more to the Credit and reputation of his family, and myself for me to come home and settle the matter between his Daughter and myself. This gives me some suspicion, that what I feared relative to a secret Oaths being taken by her, is a fact, otherwise he would not have had the assurance to wrote. To prevent any Ill consequences speedily arising should that be [the] case I have wrote him a letter filled with surprise and evasion and smothed over in such a manner that I presume he will let the matter rest for the present. His letter is inclosed in yours. I beg you to find means to convey it to him without its coming to the knowledge of any person who the letter is from. I likewise beg the contents of this may remain a secret, and the letter itself be destroyed, that no person may take an advantage from it to add to my misfortunes.[194]

193. No letters to Colonel Converse and his daughter of this date appear in the letterbook, nor is there any evidence that such letters might have been written and subsequently removed from the letterbook. The fact that the pages of the letterbook are continuously numbered is not conclusive, because this appears to have been done much later, by Gilbert's son; either Gilbert or his son might have removed offensive letters. The physical state of the letterbook indicates, however, that nothing was removed between pages 155 and 156, where letters for 19 and 31 December 1782 end and begin, respectively. Moreover, Gilbert faithfully recorded in his diary having written letters to his father and other correspondents, but there is no mention in the diary of such letters to Converse and his daughter, although the other letters in the letterbook on either side of 22 December are duly noted. The inescapable conclusion is that Gilbert was lying to Colonel Converse, and that no such letters had ever been written, much less sent.

194. The outcome of this affair involving what the editor presumes is the pregnancy of Converse's daughter, Patience, but in the letterbook unnamed, may be read in Gilbert's manuscript diary for 1783–86 at the Library of the New York State Historical Association, Cooperstown, New York. When Gilbert finally left the Army and arrived in Brookfield, 25 November 1783, he was "taken" (arrested) within a few days by warrant on "account" of Patience Converse, who was born in 1759 to James and Dorothy Converse, according to the published vital records of the town. Presumably released on

Intelligence Just received from New York informs that the British are makeing every prepiration to leave the City. If that be true and Peace is proclaimed as soon as we expect, the Army will be disbanded as soon as they quit the City. I shall repair to Brookfield, and investigate the matter and know the worst of it. Till then I wish you to advertise me of every matter either pleasing or disagreable that may have any connection with my character or Interest, that I may be enabled to form some general line of conduct.

I am etc.

Compliments

Mr. Charles Bruce
    The Colonel's Letter inclosed in this

---

bond, Gilbert visited the Converse household several times in early December before, on 9 December, settling the affair by agreeing to pay thirty pounds (about $150)—fifteen on the spot, fifteen within a year—and receiving "a full acquital from the father and Daughter," which Gilbert promptly registered with a local magistrate. Gilbert left Brookfield early in the summer of 1784. On 30 September 1784 Patience Converse married Nathan Prouty of the neighboring town of Spencer, without having first taken the usual step of recording their intention to marry; on 2 December 1784 the birth or baptism of their first child, Lydia, is recorded. Either Patience was well advanced in pregnancy when she married Nathan Prouty, or he accepted Lydia, possibly the product of the liaison between Patience and Gilbert, as his own child. If the latter is the case, Lydia must have been born well before 2 December 1784, because the pregnancy of Patience must have been manifest as early as September 1782, when John Cutler, at the behest of his father-in-law James Converse, first wrote to Gilbert about the matter. Patience Converse Prouty lived in Spencer until her death, recorded in the published Spencer vital records as the widow of Nathan in 1826, having borne fourteen children, including Lydia.

CHAPTER V

PEACE AND DEMOBILIZATION

❧

MARCH 1783 – 1786

THE LETTERS OF 24–25 MARCH, above, to Colonel Converse and brother-in-law Charles Bruce, marked an end to a difficult period of Gilbert's life. Comparing these two letters, and looking back at the first letter to Colonel Converse of 30 September 1782, we see an unattractive Benjamin Gilbert, a liar and a blusterer. He blamed others—John Cutler and his brother Isaac—for what he had originally accepted as the consequences of his own behavior. On second thought, we are not so sure. His father, whose position in the town, and as captain in Colonel Converse's militia regiment, was threatened by this scandal, apparently did not blame his son, and may have absolved him. As far as we know, Gilbert had never dared to raise the subject with his father during the months when Patience Converse grew big with what she claimed was Benjamin's child, and Daniel Gilbert may have written to his son about the affair only after she had given birth (March 1782 to January 1783, if Gilbert was indeed the father). We have reason to believe that when Patience Converse finally married, in November 1784, she was almost certainly in the late stages of another pregnancy. So we may reasonably wonder whether Gilbert, also having second thoughts after his initial, honorable confession to Colonel Converse, might indeed have been falsely accused. Without the discovery of more evidence, we will never know.

After leaving the Army at West Point and returning to Brookfield on 25 November 1783, Gilbert wrote in his diary that he "was taken with a Warrant by Hugh Cunningham [a constable] on Patience Converse's account. Went before Esquire [magistrate] Reed. Had my Tryal adjourned till Friday the ninth of December." (p. 131) Several times in the days that followed Gilbert visited Colonel Converse to negotiate a settlement. What happened on 9 December, the day set for his trial, is described in his diary: "I rode to Colonel Converses. Settled with him and his Daughter. Gave them Thirty pounds, fifteen of which I paid down, the other fifteen to be paid twelve months from the Settlement. I then took a full acquital from the father and Daughter and rode to Colonel Reeds and ackowledged it." (p. 133) The last act of this little story also appears in the diary. On 16 February 1786, shortly after marrying Mary Cornwall in Danbury, Connecticut, Gilbert rode back to Brookfield—alone—and called on Colonel Converse to pay the balance due—more than a year late. (p. 240)

The Continental Army encampment at West Point, looking north up the river, from the watercolor panorama by Pierre L'Enfant, who served on the staff of General Steuben (by permission, from the original in the Library of Congress).

Interpreting this affair, either in terms of New England *mores* or of Benjamin Gilbert's character, is not easy, although the survival of so much evidence for such ordinary people is rare. Turning a sexual difficulty into a business transaction was hardly unknown in an earlier America, although it was more common when the girl was a servant and marriage seemed out of the question. Gilbert's letters strongly suggest that both Colonel Converse and his daughter wanted and expected Gilbert to marry her, which might well have also secured the young couple's economic future, about which Gilbert worried so much in his letters. The Converses were a prominent Worcester County family, and marriage would have been a step up socially for Gilbert. His obvious lack of interest in marrying Patience suggests that there may have been reason to doubt her innocence in the affair, or to question the roles played by her brother-in-law John Cutler and his brother Isaac. Marriage would have been the easy way out.

It is possible, though not likely, that by late 1782 Gilbert had fallen in love with Molly, the

young daughter of Captain John Cornwall of Danbury. Hardly more than a child when Gilbert had met her while he was convalescing in Danbury in 1778–79, Molly would become Mrs. Gilbert in 1786 and the mother of his eleven children. Born in 1764, she nowhere in the surviving record emerges as a distinct person, except when her husband in a letter to her father described her on their New York frontier farm as having "become a hearty woman. She is able to do more business now in one week than she was in four when she left your House. Our little Dairy with the other business incident to the care of a Family employ her whol[e] time so that She is delivered from that bane of humane happiness, *Iddleness*. She feels herself contented and happy, with one Alloy which is the encroachment of the Wolves which are the constant disturbers of our Nights repose." (May 1786, *Diary*, p. 80)

Peace, negotiated in Paris, finally announced in America, and celebrated in the first letters of this last part of the letterbook, surely had delivered Benjamin Gilbert himself from "that bane of humane happiness"—idleness, because his diary, more than the letters, tell us just how idle he had been during the final months of the war, and what idleness had been doing to his character. As we have seen, Gilbert enjoyed most of the vices associated with soldiers, and this last period of the war gave him ample opportunity to engage in them. He belonged to an army stationed about fifty miles up the Hudson River from Manhattan, where a much larger, better equipped and trained British army was based. The main function of the American Army at West Point was to pin down its enemy on Manhattan, or at least, by a threatening proximity, to deter it from roaming freely through the American countryside. But this deterrent function did not normally entail a great deal of activity: some patrolling and skirmishing by detachments in lower Orange and Westchester Counties, along the edge of the no-man's land between the two armies; a certain amount of military drill and training; the inevitable guard and work "details" incident to military existence; and the equally inevitable efforts to keep the troops busy and out of trouble. But, overall, there was much idleness, with bored soldiers trying to escape their boredom.

No group in 1783 was more bored, or more idle, than the junior leaders, the sergeants and lieutenants like Gilbert, who kept the troops in order more by their presence than by anything they did. Lieutenant Gilbert and his comrades used their rank to move more freely than could ordinary soldiers in a quest for amusement—drinking, dancing, berry-picking, fishing, hunting, gambling, and whoring. His letter of 1 March 1783, above, to Captain Jonathan Stone had offered a vivid, if thinly disguised picture of the "Seraglio" at "Wyoma" (somewhere near Newburgh or the New Windsor encampment), where Gilbert spent much of his leisure and, presumably, his scanty funds between February and June. No less than fourteen visits were paid by Gilbert on "the Girls" of Wyoma, often with his friend Ensign Jonathan Wing, sometimes with Dr. James Edwards Burr Finley (son of the President of the College of New Jersey at Princeton), usually staying all night, and getting back to camp just in time for morning roll call. Only in late August, after he had received part of his back pay, when "a disagreable letter" arrived from Wyoma, probably asking him to pay his bills, did the party end.

To be fair, it must be said that there were more innocent amusements. When a minister was preaching on Sunday, Gilbert would walk to "meeting" or "divine service," just as he usually did at home in Brookfield, although he, Wing, and Finley might trek to Wyoma afterward. The previous spring, his diary records, he had "plaid at Ball severely" (p. 8, 7 April 1782), but team sports were no part of the cure for idleness in 1783. There were letters to be written and copied in the letterbook, as well as entries to be made in the diary. Three times he attended musical evenings. His regiment got drunk on news of the peace, and stayed that way for most of three days (pp. 87–88, 27–29 March), but General Washington sponsored a more genteel celebration on 19 April, when the proclamation from Congress was read, "the Independence Anthem was sung," and the great man himself toasted *Happy* and lasting *Peace*." (p. 19) And on 13 August Gilbert spent the day reading the letters of Lord Chesterfield, just the sort of paradigm of gentlemanly style whose influence shines through in some of his more strenuous literary efforts. At least once he bathed in the Hudson. Aside from occasional regimental reviews, after one of which Washington chastised the 5th Massachusetts for its unsoldierly performance, Gilbert's last active military service came in late June, when the 2nd Brigade was ordered to Philadelphia on reports of "sedition" in the Pennsylvania Line. General Robert Howe stopped the brigade near Morristown, New Jersey, and sent it back to West Point as the emergency passed (pp. 104–7).

Sometime in late June, Gilbert wrote the last, undated letter to his father, No. 11, with its unforgettable picture of impoverished American soldiers, "those brave heroes, the deliverers of my Country," drifting down the Hudson to seek employment on the British transports evacuating the British Army from New York, getting in street brawls with the Tories but being cheered on by Hessian soldiers, many of whom would desert rather than return to Germany. On 1 September Gilbert finally got leave, "for the recovery of my health," and set off to see his friends in Danbury, much closer to West Point than Brookfield.

At Danbury, he stayed with the Hoyts, who had nursed him through the bad months in 1779, but he spent afternoons drinking tea with the Cornwalls, the family of his future wife. Danbury was far more amusing than the army encampment at New Windsor. Gilbert rode to New Haven, and met his first cousin Benjamin J. Gilbert, a Yale student, at the College commencement (p. 119, 10 September). He watched the local militia train, and "saw a Capital Horse race" (p. 122, 6–7 October). Through what must have been euphoric autumn weeks of falling in love, there were parties and balls, for which he faithfully recorded every dance with Mary Cornwall (pp. 124–29). Late November, winter approaching, he set out for Brookfield, to see his own family, and to keep his rendezvous with Colonel Converse.

At Brookfield, aside from the Converse affair, there were debts to be paid and collected, friends and relatives to be visited, a horse and saddle to be bought, a trip to Boston to settle his army pay, and farm chores to be done. But his wild oats were still not quite sown. Gilbert, it must be said, followed a Puritan tradition in being a faithful recorder of his own lapses; whether guilt, or some compulsion to keep good records, made him do it, his diary lets us watch his last fling before settling down a few months later to school teaching, farming, and marriage. Shaking off whatever embarrassment he may have felt about the Converse scandal, he renewed old acquaintances around town, including visits to the home of Colonel Jeduthan Baldwin, a former Continental officer of artillery and engineers. Baldwin had a daughter Elizabeth (Betsy), six years younger than Gilbert, and the nocturnal visits to Colonel Baldwin's, and the diary entries, "L^d·w^h Bal^d" leave little doubt as to what was happening between 24 December 1783 and 20 February 1784. During the same winter in western Massachusetts, as he traveled about seeing friends, there are cryptic, suspicious entries of evenings spent "agreably" (a favorite adjective applied to earlier evenings at Wyoma) at the widow Porter's or with Miss Baldwin, and of lodging with Mrs. Carter, where he spent the evening "agreeably in Company of the Young People of that Neighbourhood," and later "L^d· w^h Cr Car^r" (pp. 136–45). Clearly, Benjamin Gilbert was no saint, but perhaps he was no worse than a normal young man, his twenties spent in the corrupting ambience of an army at war.

The rest of the story, carrying far beyond the last letter to his father from West Point, is summarily recounted in the Introduction, above, and may here be concluded. He rode northeast from Brookfield, to Rutland, to visit his old family friend and former commander, General Rufus Putnam, in March 1784, and spent three days letting Putnam teach him surveying (pp. 148–49). After three lines of undeciphered shorthand or code on 22 March, the diary virtually— and uncharacteristically—lapses until he left Brookfield in June 1784.

No evidence exists to suggest that Gilbert ever hesitated about leaving Brookfield. Although numerous relatives and friends lived in or near the town, Gilbert had written bitterly to his father of having "so many enemies" in Brookfield who wished to "destroy" him (30 January 1783, above); the town may have lost any hold it once had on him. Opportunity was also limited there. The son of what appears to have been the less favored heir of his grandfather Benjamin, Gilbert could hope for no more than a modest inheritance (his father Daniel died in 1824, age 95). Gilbert's birthdate had combined with the outbreak of war to deprive him of any chance at the advantages enjoyed by his first cousins, Benjamin Joseph and Daniel, who graduated from Yale and Dartmouth, respectively, and who had successful legal careers. Perhaps conclusive in his decision was Brookfield itself. As late as 1798, before shoemaking energized its economy, a contemporary observer described Brookfield as backward and chronically depressed—"rural beyond almost any other town in the region"; sparsely populated, its houses were little better than unpainted, crudely furnished shacks; no one owned a carriage or wagon, and the congregation froze through winter Sunday meetings. Aside from a few part-time blacksmiths, tanners, millers, and the inevitable tavern-keepers, everyone in Brookfield lived by farming.[195] During eight years in the Army, Gilbert had seen some of the rest of America, and presumably the war had prepared him to leave primitive Brookfield behind.

After a brief visit to Danbury, Gilbert headed north to Albany, where he delivered a letter to General Philip Schuyler, the father-in-law of Alexander Hamilton, and then turned west until he reached Warrens Bush (Warren today), just northwest of Otsego Lake. There he began his new life by teaching school, and soon bought a farm near Cherry Valley, at a settlement originally called Newtown Martin, soon renamed Middlefield, just east of Otsego Lake—the "Glimmerglass" of James Fenimore Cooper's Leatherstocking Tales. His education and knowledge of surveying were his survival kit as he pieced together a new existence on the frontier. In

195. Temple, *Brookfield*, pp. 265–67.

this part of the diary we learn, more than from anything he wrote during the war, what a tough and determined man the thirty-year-old Gilbert had become. Winter journeys back to Danbury and Brookfield, the carefully recorded struggle to make his farm pay, left no place for assignations with local belles. He sometimes went to meeting on Sunday, as of old, once reading a sermon himself when there was no preacher, visiting the "Universalians" on another occasion. He brought a new wife back from Danbury, in 1786, stopping in Albany (but not at Brookfield) to pay off the mortgage on the farm.

In October 1786 he was commissioned adjutant of Colonel Cannon's regiment of New York militia, and we can follow him through the 1790s in the *Otsego Herald*, eleven years as sheriff of Otsego County, three terms assemblyman in the New York State legislature, as well as holder of numerous local and county offices. The Masonic Lodge, whose original building still stands in Cooperstown, and the Federalist party, were his chief interests beyond farm and family. As one who had done his share of complaining during the war about politicians who failed to support the military, Gilbert is caught by the historical record acting like a politician, voting against a legislative appropriation for the fortification of New York harbor during the war crisis with France in 1798 because his political enemy, Aaron Burr, had sponsored the bill.[196] At some point he and Mary Cornwall Gilbert may have become Baptists; they are buried in the Baptist churchyard. Whether Sheriff Benjamin Gilbert had actually stuffed the ballot box in 1792, as some Republicans thought, to ensure the election of Mr. John Jay as Governor, has no certain answer, but the impulsive, aggressive, not always scrupulous young American who can be discerned with some clarity in these letters and diaries might well have seen fit to do so.

A single life can seldom do more than exemplify the period of history in which it was lived. Yet, in the specificity of a life that is fairly typical, we are able to see and better understand the broad general statements which historians use to make sense of the past. The life of Benjamin Gilbert offers just such a graphic, specific example of general patterns and processes in the formative period of American national society. From a primitive but cohesive background in rural New England, Gilbert kept the forms though not the deeper spiritual faith of the intense Protestantism of his ancestors. Many Sundays were spent at religious meetings, walking miles to get there, but on other Sundays—when there were no services, or there was business to be done—Gilbert let the day pass without any recorded sign of distress. His father's generation, when waging war against French and Indians, had often used their diaries to deplore military lapses from true Christian behavior, especially on the Sabbath, but Gilbert's letters and diaries strongly suggest that Puritanism, in his life, had ceased to be much more than engrained tradition. The Providential God of Cotton Mather, who saw holy meaning in every earthly event, had given way for Gilbert to the benign Watchmaker of Benjamin Franklin.

196. *Otsego Herald: or, Western Advertiser*, 11 October 1798.

Faith, in the life of Benjamin Gilbert, appears to have focused less on God than on American destiny. Eight years of arduous, ill-paid military service, in which he had spent most of his youth, seem never to have shaken his faith in the justness of the American struggle, or in the promise of the American future; indeed, devoting most of his young life to the cause may have made his attachment to that cause unbreakable. Seen in the light of his own personal commitment to the emerging nation, the less appealing side of his character—the narcissistic quality of so many of the letters, the provincial aping of European attitudes and style, the occasional lack of honesty—seem minor, and serve mainly to confirm and illustrate what so many contemporary observers saw as the essential American Revolutionary—energetic, ambitious, boastful, and desperately eager for external approval. Pulled by the war out of New England, Gilbert learned that the world was not bounded by Brookfield and Boston; New York, New Jersey, Pennsylvania, Maryland, and Virginia were distinct cultures, but the war had taught him to see them as parts of the larger, paramount whole that was "America." The strongly nationalist program, articulated forcefully by his contemporary, Alexander Hamilton, first as an Army colonel, later as leader of the Federalist party, appealed to Lieutenant Gilbert's war-formed consciousness, and left him with little evident sympathy for the decentralizing, libertarian agenda of Jeffersonianism. Freedom of course he surely valued, freedom to move, to learn and to strive, as well as to take an active part in public life, but freedom for Gilbert had fused with his faith in the nation. The freedom that served him so well after 1783 was simply the defining characteristic of a strong, independent United States, and the predictable result of its war for independence. Not for him was the perceived tension and conflict between a strong nation and personal liberty, a tension that troubled so many followers of Thomas Jefferson.

In the end, the most remarkable feature of his life may be the care and candor with which he recorded his Revolutionary experience, as well as the good fortune that preserved this record to our own time. Very few Revolutionary soldiers, not even better educated officers, left a good, contemporary account of what they did, saw, and thought. None to my knowledge left such an intimate, personally revealing record as did Gilbert. We would like to know still more about him, particularly about his part in the war before 1778, and about the connection between his wartime experience and his postwar politics, but in an age when some of the most insistent, and intractable, questions being raised by historians concern the mentality of "ordinary" people, we are exceptionally lucky to have the letters and diaries of Benjamin Gilbert.

New Windsor   26th March 1783

Honored Sire

His Excellency has this morning favoured us with a letter which he received last Night from Philedelphia, the contents of which informs that a packet is arived from France which assures us that a General peace was signed by all the Billigerant powers of Europe and America on the 20th of January last, and that Hostillities wer to cease in America the 20th of this Instant. The British troops are prepareing to leave New York. As soon as they have affected that, the American Army will be disbanded and return to those home's from which they have been absent for a long time with no other View than to obtain that Peace and Independence which is now ceeded to us.

This assurance of Peace will put a stop to location in this state, consequently my plan must fall.[197] If you have not disposed of my Note agreable to my request in No. 5 [17 March, above] I wish you not to do it till you here further from me, for in all probabillity, state security's will rise immediately after the peace. If you have, or have Received any other monies please to send it on agreable to my instructions in No. 5.

I have many more things I could say, but want of time prevents.

I must conclude

Captain D Gilbert   No. 6

N Windsor   7th April 1783

Honored Sire

The bearer of this Doctor Hale[198] will call on you. If you have any monies in your posession belonging to me please to deliver it to the Doctor and it will meet with a saft conveyance. If you have deposited any monies with Captains Hitchcock or Lincoln that is not sent on, wish you to put it into the Doctors power to obtain it and perhaps it we be conveyed to me sooner than by any other method.

If you have disposed of my Notes, wish you not to do it, as the 5th and 6th Articles of the peace puts a stop to all business of the kind, that I proposed to enter into.[199] It will be needless

---

197. This was Gilbert's plan to join Captain Nathan Goodale of Brookfield in buying lands near Albany due for confiscation as Loyalist property in March 1783. See the letter to his father of 18 January 1783, above, and his last letter with note, below.

198. Probably Dr. William Hale, whose father had moved to Brookfield from Newbury c. 1715. Temple, *Brookfield*, p. 611.

199. See the previous letter and note.

for to enter into particulars relative to Peace. Undoubtedly your papers gives a fuller detail of those matters, than I posibly could do in this letter. You may rely on seing me in Brookfield by the first of June perhaps sooner.

    Compliments etc.

Captain Gilbert
No. 7

TO HIS FATHER

N.Windsor   May 5th 1783

Honored Sire—

    I thank you for your favour of the 22d Ultimo. I received it by the hand of Josiah White. Was extreemly happy to here you and your family was in health. It gives me not a little satisfaction to be informed by your letter that my Number 6 [of 26 March, above] forwarded by Capt. White came to your hands early enough to prevent the sale of my notes. I think it is for my interest not to sell any of them till the price is greater, which I think will be very soon.

    If I am not rong in my calculations I have in your posession a sheeps wool Note which was payable last March. I wish you to send it to Boston for consolidation the first convenient opportunity.

    Every thing is prepairing for a great day of rejoiceing in Camp. A fu-de-joye, an illumination, and a great display of fire works will be the principal actions worthy of notice on that Day.

    It remains an uncertainty when the Army will be disbanded, as it will not be safe to quit the field and leave Carlton[200] in possision of New York and he appears to move but slowley.

    Compliments etc.

Captain D Gilbert
No. 8

TO HIS COUSIN DANIEL GOULD

N. Windsor   6th May 1783

Dear Sir

    I congratulate you on the return of *Peace*. It crowns in happy maner all our Labours, and is a blissing if truly realised will promote the happiness of every subject of it. The prospect of speedily returning to the walks of private life fills my heart with raptures, and while I anticipate

---

200. Sir Guy Carleton, who had succeeded Sir Henry Clinton as Commander-in-Chief of the British Army in North America.

the Joies that awaits us, I cannot but advertise you of the anxious thoughts which at present fills my breast.

A state of suspence must be allowed by all to be the most disagreeable of any short of real misery. That the former is my case you will readily grant when you consider the following reasons. The definitive treaty is not signed or if signed is not come to hand. Carlton is in possesion of New York and no prospects of his speedily leaving it. To quit the field before our coast is clear would argue a total want of sense. Neither shall we, but we remain inactive without imployment, and under such restrictions that we can make no arrangements for Domestic life. Thus I spend my time in idleness under a continual agjutation of mind, praying for a speedy desolution of the Army.

I am Dear sir Yours etc.
B Gilbert

Mr. D. Gould
    Western

TO HIS FATHER

New Windsor   May 16th 1783

Honored Sire

Your favour of the 22d Ultimo came safte to hand by the care of Doctor Hale. Am happy to here of the health of yourself and family.

Perhaps you will be surprised when I inform you that time never passed more disagreable than it does at present.

A state of suspence is truly the most unhappy of any short of real misery, and that is mine now in the fullest sence of the word. For some time past I have been anticipating the pleasure and Enjoyments that are to be found in the walks of private life, and hoped and wished that every new day would bring the happy news of the definitive treaty being signed (that I might immediately retire from the field, and Join with my friends in all the amusements of domestic Life,) but alas! it is not arived. Neither have we any great expectations of being discharged this four weeks, should it arive the present hour, for the convention Troops in Virginia, and those taken with Lord Cornwallis, are to be marched to New York for embarcation, and every objection that can be offered (on the part of the British) to delay their departure is made. Those circumstances with many others must convince the weakest minds, that it would be inconsistant with sound pollicy to disband our army while so many of those who have been our open, and now are our secret enemies, remain in arms on the Continent. It is further hinted by some from New York tho' not openly declared, that *Sir* Guy [Carleton] has orders not to leave New York

[105]

untill Congress has fully complyed with the 5th and 6th Articles of the Peace, and that he is collecting all the British Troops in America, to that garison under pretence of makeing a general Embarcation, and if that the States do not comply with the recommendation of Congress respecting the Loyalists, that he will put himself in a posture of defence and wait the direction of Parliment.[201]

The foregoing reasons together with the uncertainty when I shall be free and what business should I go into was I free, makes time pass very slow and disagreable. I could say many thingss more but shall only add that it is a general time of Health.

B Gilbert

Captain Gilbert No. 9

TO HIS FATHER

[c. 6 June 1783]

Honored Sir

In consequence of the late proclimation and Resolve of Congress, all men for the War are now furloughed, and all the Officers except enough to command the three years men, who will form six Regiments, five of Infantry (four of which belongs to Massachusetts) and one of Artillery. The fifth Regiment of Infantry will be composed of the few remaining three Years men belonging to New Hampshire and Connecticut. The Maryland, Jersy, and New York Lines have already quited the field, and those of Massachusetts and the other States, will be gone in two days. My Juniority does not entitle me to command in either of the four Regiments. I am obliged to quit the field whether I choose or not. But not haveing received one Copper of money from the public since I left Brookfield, and the small sum you sent me being expended for necessaries, I am obliged to remain in the neighbourhood of Camp untill I can get my accounts settled with the public. The Ballance in my favour I must sell to enable me to pay my debts and get money to carry me Home.

The six Regiments mentioned above will continue no longer in the field than till the definitive treaty arives, at which time there will be a final desolution of our Army.

As I am about to retire from the Military Theatre to walks of private life, without any cash, or the means of obtaining any, I find it necessary to make some arrangments for my future support, but in what way or manner I am totally at a loss. You will perhaps say that labour

201. The fifth article required Congress to recommend that the States restore confiscated property; this proved to be a dead letter. The sixth article forbade any further prosecution of Loyalists or confiscation of their property.

constantly followed will yeald me an ample subsistance. This I grant but at the same time I know my constitution is so far spent, that I am not able to earn the one half per Month or day that I was before the war.

You wrote me some time ago that Reuben Gilbert would bring some cattle to you, to pay the debt he owes me. If he should bring stock of any kind this sumer, previous to my return, If you have pasture that you can keep them without injuring your own stock, wish you to do it till you herre further from me.

Please to pardon the unconnectedness of this letter when I assure you I fall but little short of a delirum. Perhaps I shall write again before I se you. If I should I hope it will be more regular.

Compliments etc.

No. 10
Captain Gilbert

TO HIS BROTHER-IN-LAW CHARLES BRUCE

[10 June 1783]

Dear Sir

It is impossible for me to paint to you the disagreable feelings which I have undergone for four or five days past. Those brave men who were for the war and who have been fighting from four to eight years in defense of their Country and for the preservation of its liberty, are now discharged the service, and are retiring from the field of Glory with Joy in their countenances, but poverty in their pockets. Not one man to twenty of them, has a single farthing to support him on his passage to his friends, but must be under the necessaty of beging of those people for the protection of whose liberties and property they have so long fought—an unprecedented piece of ingratitude. If we search the records of heaven, or all the annals of the antint or modern wars, we cannot find a parallel instance of inhumanity. If this Continent and its inhabitants were worth fighting for, one could not be so ungenerous as to suppose it would not reward its protectors. I am at some times almost tempted to wish I had not lived to se the day when those brave heroes the deliverers of my Country should be drove from the field of Glory without one farthing of reward for their services. Where is the Justice, where is the propriety of the Army's bearing the whole burthen of the war.

I am sure, nay I dare assert it for the truth that, if the Citisans the Legislature and the Civil Goverment in General had been disposed to share the burthen in common with the Army, we should not have been compelled after Eight years faithfull service to look up to those people for a support for whose protection we have so often fought and Bled. The subject is so painfull

I defer giving my sentiments further till my circumstances shall permit me to wait on you, which if I wait for relief from the public, I fear will be some time first.

Compliments etc.

10 June 1783
Mr. Charles Bruce

TO HIS FATHER

[late June 1783]

Honered Sire

Since writing No. 10 Lieutenant Smith who had proposed to remain in service altering his mind and wishing to retire proposed to make an exchange with me. My circumstances being such that I could not possibly get home at present, thought proper to exchange with him and he retires. The 5th Regiment being reduced I am arranged in the 3d where you will please to direct any letters you shall write me. My Command will continue no longer than till the definitive treaty arives, at which time a final desolution of our Army will take place.

A large number of Transports have arived at New York from Brittan to carry the Troops home, a very great number of Soldiers that have been fourloughed have gone to New York with a view of Shipping themselves on Board Vessels for employment. But [not?] getting immediate employment, they are roveing about the City, where frequent quarels happen between them and the refugees.[202] Our Soldiers meeting with every protection and assistance from the Hessians they flogg the Refugees every engagement.

Desertion provails among the Hessians, they are determined, a great number of them, not to return but say they are so much prejudiced in favour of the soil, Goverment and Inhabitants of America that they mean to become Inhabitants of it.

If the Treasurer has begun to pay the Interest due on Consolidated securities wish you to make application for the payment of what is due on mine.

No. 11
Captain D. Gilbert
New Windsor

202. "Refugee" was a generic term for American Loyalist.

Benjamin Gilbert was Born May 31st 1755 and died January 18th 1828. At his death he was 72 years, 7 months, 18 days old. His native place was the Town of Brookfield in the County of Worcester, and State of Massachusetts.

Mary S. Gilbert the said Benjamin Gilbert's wife, was born January 13th 1764. Her native place was the Town of Danbury County of Litchfield Connecticut State.

This note was made by their son Daniel Gilbert, August 29th 1841 — the said Mary S. Gilbert then Residing near said Daniel Gilbert's in the Village of Clarksville Otsego County State of New York.

APPENDIX

THE PENSION APPLICATION
OF BENJAMIN GILBERT

❦

FEDERAL LEGISLATION IN 1818, revised in 1820, created service pensions for veterans of the Revolutionary War. Previously, only those maimed in the war were eligible for a Federal pension. Thousands of survivors, including Benjamin Gilbert, applied under the 1818 law, and his affidavit is valuable for its description of his military service in his own words. His application was approved, so that Gilbert, until his death, and his widow for years thereafter, enjoyed the benefits of the first Federal welfare program.[203]

> I certify that on the 19th of April 1775 in the evening I marched for Lexington, and entered into Captain Peter Harwood's Company in Colonel Leonard's [Larned's] Regiment and served in said Regiment during the whole Campaign of 1775.
>
> That in January 1776 I inlisted in Captain Peter Harwood's Company in Colonel Leonard's [Larned's] Regiment and served in Said Regiment the whole Company [Campaign] of 1776. That in January 1777 I inlisted into Captain Daniel Shays Company as a Serjant in the 5th Massachusetts Regiment commanded by Rufus Putnam Colonel and served in said Regiment as a Serjant during the Campaign of 1777–1778 and part of the Campaign of 1779 when on the 26th day of November 1779 I was appointed by the bord of War at Boston as an Ensign in Colonel Rufus Putnam's regiment, and was commissioned on the 27th day of August 1781 an Ensign in the fifth Massachusetts Regiment in the Army of the United States by Thomas McKean President of Congress, That on the 17th day of April 1782 I was Commissioned a Lieutenant in the Massachusetts Line in the Army of the United States by Elias Boudinot Esquire President of Congress, and that I continued as a Lieutenant in said Army untill the Close of the year 1783 when the army was disbanded. Then from the 19th day of April 1775 to the Close of the year 1783 I constantly continued to be mustered, do duty, and receive pay according to the different Situation in which the regulation of the Army placed me, and that I now reside in the Town of Middlefield County of Otsego and State of New York, and have resided in the said Town upwards of thirty four years, and am at this date upwards of sixty two years of Age.
>
> Benjamin Gilbert

---

203. *The Revolution Remembered: Eyewitness Accounts of the War of Independence*, edited by John C. Dann (Chicago: Univ. of Chicago Press, 1980), provides a fuller account of the pension system as well as a selection from the more interesting affidavits drawn from the thousands of pension files, alphabetically arranged, in the U.S. National Archives.

ACKNOWLEDGEMENTS

THE GENEROSITY of Mr. Benjamin D. Gilbert, a direct descendant of Lieutenant Benjamin Gilbert, and the enthusiasm of Dr. John C. Dann, Director of the William L. Clements Library, have facilitated editing and publishing the letterbook at every step of the process. Similarly, the work of Rebecca Symmes in editing the first part of Gilbert's diary made my own task much easier, and readers are referred to her *A Citizen-Soldier in the American Revolution: The Diary of Benjamin Gilbert in Massachusetts and New York* (Cooperstown, 1980), for essential background on Gilbert's personality, experience, and associations. Daniel Porter, Director of the New York State Historical Association at Cooperstown, where both portions of the Gilbert diary are housed, was hospitable as well as helpful in providing access to the second, unpublished portion of the diary, while Amy Barnum and Wendell Tripp of the Association provided important information on Gilbert's postwar political career.

Howard Peckham, former Director of the Clements Library, gave the book an early, careful reading, and was, as he invariably has been, generous in sharing his great knowledge of the American Revolution.

Roy Kiplinger worked diligently and efficiently with me in the process of transcribing and annotating the letterbook, shared his thoughts on Gilbert's attitudes and motives, and did the index. My undergraduate seminar, asked to examine portions of the letterbook, offered empathetically youthful perspectives on Gilbert's behavior; I am particularly grateful to James Doyle. Professor Ira Gruber of Rice University was a valuable consultant on obscure portions of the letters and diaries. David Bosse, Curator of Maps at the Clements Library, was of great help with illustrations. Thanks also to John Harriman of the Clements staff and to Mary Erwin of the University of Michigan Press, and to staff members of Hasbrouck House at Newburgh, New York, and at the nearby New Windsor Cantonment, for help in our vain effort to locate the place identified by Gilbert as "Wyoma."

My wife, Arlene, who did part of the research during our visit to Cooperstown, and who listened patiently to each new thought about our young hero from Brookfield, has earned, as ever, my special gratitude.

JOHN SHY

SELECTED BIBLIOGRAPHY

SOURCES

Brookfield, Massachusetts, town records from 1719, have been microfilmed by the Genealogical Library of the Church of Jesus Christ of Latter-day Saints. Film No. 868522.

Dann, John C., ed. *The Revolution Remembered: Eyewitness Accounts of the War of Independence*. Chicago: The University of Chicago Press, 1980.

Ewald, Johann. *Diary of the American War*. Edited and translated by Joseph P. Tustin. New Haven: Yale University Press, 1979.

Gilbert, Benjamin. Manuscript diary, 22 March 1782 – 23 December 1786. Library of the New York State Historical Association. Cooperstown, New York. See Symmes, below.

Morris, Robert. *The Papers of Robert Morris*. Edited by E. James Ferguson and others. Pittsburgh: The University of Pittsburgh Press, 1973—.

Symmes, Rebecca D., ed. *Citizen-Soldier in the American Revolution: The Diary of Benjamin Gilbert in Massachusetts and New York*. Cooperstown: The New York State Historical Association, 1980.

Tyler, Royall. *The Contrast. A Comedy; in Five Acts*. Philadelphia: Prichard and Hall, 1790.

U.S. National Archives. "Selected Records from Revolutionary War Pension and Bounty-Land-Warrant Application Files." Microcopy No. 805. 898 microfilm rolls. Washington, DC: 1969.

Washington, George. *The Writings of George Washington from the Original Manuscript Sources*, edited by John C. Fitzpatrick. 39 volumes. Washington, DC: U.S. Government Printing Office, 1931–1944.

SECONDARY AND REFERENCE WORKS

Carp, E. Wayne. *To Starve the Army at Pleasure: Continental Army Administration and American Political Culture, 1775–1783*. Chapel Hill: The University of North Carolina Press, 1984.

Daughters of the American Revolution. *DAR Patriot Index*. Washington, DC: National Society of the Daughters of the American Revolution, 1966. With two Supplements, 1969 and 1973.

Dexter, Franklin Bowditch. *Biographical Notices of Graduates of Yale College.* 6 volumes. New Haven: H. Holt and Co., 1913.

Ferguson, E. James. *The Power of the Purse: A History of Public Finance, 1776–1790.* Chapel Hill: The University of North Carolina Press, 1961.

Fielding, Henry. *The History of Tom Jones, A Foundling.* 6 volumes. London: A. Millar, 1749. Many later editions.

Hall, Van Beck. *Politics Without Parties: Massachusetts, 1780–1791.* Pittsburgh: The University of Pittsburgh Press, 1972.

Hammond, Jabez, D. *The History of Political Parties in the State of New York*, 4th ed. 2 volumes. Buffalo: Phinney and Co., 1850.

Heitman, Francis B. *Historical Register of Officers of the Continental Army*, rev. ed. Washington, DC: Rare Book Publishing Co., 1914.

Henretta, James A., and Nobles, Gregory H. *Evolution and Revolution: American Society, 1600–1820.* Lexington: D.C. Heath, 1987.

Higginbotham, Don. *The War of American Independence: Military Attitudes, Policies, and Practice, 1763–1789.* New York: Macmillan, 1971.

Hufeland, Otto. *Westchester County During the American Revolution, 1775–1783.* White Plains: Westchester County Historical Society, 1926.

Jedrey, Christopher. *The World of John Cleaveland.* New York: W. W. Norton, 1979.

Kohn, Richard H. "The Inside History of the Newburgh Conspiracy: America and the Coup d'Etat," *William and Mary Quarterly*, 3d ser., XXVII (1970), pp. 187–220.

Massachusetts, Commonwealth of. *Massachusetts Soldiers and Sailors of the Revolutionary War.* 17 volumes. Boston: 1896–1908.

Minot, George R. *The History of the Insurrections, in Massachusetts, in the Year MDCLXXXVI, and the Rebellion Consequent Thereon.* Worcester: Isaiah Thomas, 1788.

National Genealogical Society. *Index of Revolutionary War Pension Applications in the National Archives.* Washington, DC: 1976.

Nelson, Paul David. "Horatio Gates at Newburgh, 1783: A Misunderstood Role," *William and Mary Quarterly*, 3d ser., XXIX (1972), pp. 143–58.

Newcomer, Lee N. *The Embattled Farmers; A Massachusetts Countryside in the American Revolution.* New York: King's Crown Press, 1953.

Peckham, Howard H. *The Toll of Independence: Engagements and Battle Casualties of the Revolution.* Chicago: The University of Chicago Press, 1974.

Peckham, Howard H. *Treason of the Blackest Dye.* Ann Arbor: The William L. Clements Library, 1958.

Risch, Erna. *Supplying Washington's Army*. Washington, DC: Center of Military History, U.S. Army, 1981.

Royster, Charles. *A Revolutionary People at War: The Continental Army and American Character, 1775–1783*. Chapel Hill: The University of North Carolina Press, 1979.

Shipton, Clifford K. *Sibley's Harvard Graduates: Biographical Sketches of Those Who Attended Harvard College*, begun by J. L. Sibley. Cambridge: Harvard University Press, 1873–.

Smith, Frank, ed. *Memorials of the Massachusetts Society of the Cincinnati*. Boston: George H. Ellis Co., 1931.

Szatmary, David P. *Shays' Rebellion: The Making of an Agrarian Insurrection*. Amherst: The University of Massachusetts Press, 1980.

Taylor, Robert J. *Western Massachusetts in the Revolution*. Providence: Brown University Press, 1954.

Temple, Josiah H. *The History of North Brookfield, Massachusetts*. North Brookfield: published by the town, 1887.

Van Doren, Carl. *Mutiny in January*. New York: Viking Press, 1943.

Van Doren, Carl. *Secret History of the American Revolution*. New York: Viking Press, 1941.

Wallace, Willard M. *Traitorous Hero: The Life and Fortunes of Benedict Arnold*. New York: Harper, 1954.

Ward, Christopher. *The War of the Revolution*. Edited by John R. Alden. 2 volumes. New York: Macmillan, 1952.

INDEX